Momma
Do You Hear My Cry?

The Next Chapter

Momma
Do You Hear My Cry?
The Next Chapter

Makayla Townsell

G.Battles PUBLISHING.com

Omaha, Nebraska

MOMMA DO YOU HEAR MY CRY? THE NEXT CHAPTER

G.Battles Publishing
www.gbattlespublishing.com

Publishing Inquiries:
c/o Concierge Publishing Services
4822 South 133rd Street
Omaha, NE 68137

Paperback ISBN: 978-1-936840-99-1
Mobi ISBN: 978-1-936840-68-7
EPUB ISBN: 978-1-936840-69-4
LCCN: 2019931601

Library of Congress Cataloging in Publication
data on file with the publisher

Publishing and production provided by
Concierge Publishing Services, www.conciergemarketing.com

Printed in the USA

10 9 8 7 6 5 4 3 2

"You can't heal what you are afraid to reveal."

"Forgiveness does not require reconnection."

This book is inspired by and based off of the true story of Makayla's life; however, names and situations have been changed and/or altered to protect the innocent.

The purpose of this book is to reflect on how family secrets can affect generations of families, how drugs and the street life can have an effect on innocent children, and how children see and understand more than we can ever imagine. By sharing her story, Makayla hopes that other young girls can relate, and perhaps her story can help raise awareness to what people don't know or may not understand. Makayla envisions Momma Do You Hear My Cry? The Next Chapter *to be a conversation starter, a healing process, a voice for those who are too afraid to use their own, and a way for people to face their own truths, however ugly they might be.*

Through the mind of a young girl, Kayla,
Momma Do You Hear My Cry? The Next Chapter
will share the truths, struggles, trials, and tribulations
Makayla Townsell experienced.

CONTENTS

DEDICATION

I dedicate this book to the many young women like myself, who have been a victim to family curses/secrets, and who suffered from the crack epidemic in the 80s. It's hard to be vulnerable and let people into your life. For them to judge you and create an opinion. I was told that no one can tell your story better than you can. I learned people will judge you no matter what. So, I will be the one who depicts how my story will be told. People tend to think they know you because they know *of* you, but they have no idea the story you hold inside.

This book is dedicated to breaking cycles and family curses that are carried from generation to generation in families. Some girls have no choice but to grow up fast, and this book is dedicated to them. Most importantly this book is dedicated to healing and forgiving.

Momma, I forgive you for all the wrong you did while you were suffering from addiction. I know you love me, and that you are fighting a disease. One day I hope that you will win the battle. I love you. To my daddy, I forgive you for not being there. You were young and you had to grow up yourself. I know that you love me, you just had to grow.

Love Always, your daughter.

To my family I forgive you for not seeing the pain I went through growing up. I don't blame you because I worked hard to cover up the pain. To all the men I've come across, I forgive you as well. You all helped me to learn and to grow.

Most importantly, I dedicate this book to my four children Lafayette, LaMar'e, Kevin, and Kaylee. You all are the air that I breathe, and I will always have your back as long as I have breath in my body. I'm not perfect, but I will always do my best.

Love Always, Momma.

INTRO (GRADUATION)

————— ᐱ —————

According to naysayers, and statistics Kayla would not be walking across the stage. The stereotype was that she was would bare children, lose custody of them, and be addicted to drugs just like her mother.

That Spring day in would be one she'd remember for years to come. The day that she would prove so many wrong. It was the day she was graduating from high school. While many had doubted her, there was a long road to get her to that point. Leaving the ninth grade with zero credits and being a grade behind, she even doubted herself many times, but she kept pushing. She told herself she was going to graduate high school. Kayla couldn't even brag on the good grades she was receiving in her classes because, she was too ashamed. There she was a high school senior but all her progress reports, and reports cards stated she was in fact a junior.

It was shocking to others that the day in spring of 2001 became the first day of the rest of her life, and she was claiming it.. She had been anticipating that day for a while, so it was definitely a big deal. Kayla had exactly enough credits to graduate, nothing more, nothing less. However, she was going to walk that stage on time with her class as a Central High School Eagle. On the 22nd of May; in 2001, Kayla's special day had finally arrived.

With Kayla inviting damn near her whole family, she had to hustle together enough tickets. She was only allowed three free tickets and was eligible to get an additional seven if purchased. This was not enough for her large family, so she tapped into her creative side and went around school asking her classmates to sell their leftover tickets. Including kids who unfortunately aren't graduating the current high school year. This method seemed to have worked for Kayla, and it was a big deal—and one in which she wasn't playing any games.

No one was more proud of Kayla then her father, Ray. "Good Morning, Kayla! What are you doing? Come outside" he told her. He was ecstatic. Ray rarely showed emotion, but that day he couldn't hide it even if he wanted to. He definitely was in rare form and out of character that day. His baby girl was graduating high school. She wasn't a baby anymore, but to him she would always be a baby, his baby.

Barely awake, Kayla went outside and her father jumped out of the car, just grinning from ear to ear. Anyone who knew him would know that these actions were rare. He hardly ever smiled, let alone showed emotions. He embraced Kayla with a hug and he handed her an envelope. When Kayla opened it, she pulled out a card. As she opened the card, twenty-dollar bills started falling out. Trying to act unbothered, Kayla read the card, acting as if the money wasn't a big deal. When in reality, all she could think about how much money was there.

Kayla was completely caught off guard, so all she could say was "thank you". She wanted to embrace him with a huge hug, but their relationship wasn't like that.

"Thank you," replied Kayla with a big smile showing off her dimples. Kayla returned inside the house, full of excitement.

She darted toward Jackie's room. She squealed, "LOOK!" while hopping and spreading money all across the bed. Jackie was just as thrilled as Kayla, they both realized they had never had that much money at once. After counting, it came out to be $1,000 in $20 bills. "I wish it was graduation everyday," said Kayla. They burst out into laughter.

Time was ticking, Kayla had much to do to get ready for graduation. Avery had finally arrived to do Kayla's hair. They spent most of the afternoon fucking off, smoking, and joking around, so it took the majority of the day.

"It's graduation day, aye" Avery kept chanting and dancing. She probably was the second happiest after Ray that Kayla was going to be graduating. She had been cheering Kayla on damn near her whole life. Kayla could still hear the voice in her head saying, "You can do it" every time she doubted herself and wanted to give up.

The whole crew was so excited for Kayla that they couldn't contain themselves that day. They were celebrating like graduation had already taken place. Before her hair was even finished, Ray had stopped by again with another envelope filled with another $1,000 in twenties. Kayla was shocked-- she was suddenly in the money and felt like she had just won the lottery.

Avery finished her work on Kayla's hair, and then it was time to pick up Kay. Kayla had been prepping Kay for this special day for weeks prior, so she would understand how important it was to her daughter that she be there. Kayla had talked to her earlier to remind her again to be ready. As Kayla parked in front of Pete's house on 16th and Maple and honked the horn. A few minutes passed, and Kay still hadn't come out. So Kayla honked again and waited—still no one.

Kayla banged on the door "Momma, Momma!" she screamed. Still no answer. She ran to the side of the building to Pete's entrance and knocked on his door. After several minutes, he came to the door, going through his routine of first peeking his beady eyes through the curtain to see who was there. Although, he knew very well who it was, he cracked the door open, peeking through like Kayla was a stranger, even though he had known her since she was a little girl.

"Where's Momma?" Kayla said, Irritated by his reluctance to come to the door.

"She was sitting on the porch earlier, she must have went around the corner," he said.

Kayla was irritated. She had spoken to Kay several times about this important day, and they had made a plan. Once again Kay was letting her daughter down. "This is some bullshit," Kayla mumbled under her breath. "Okay" she said to Pete then jumped back in the running car. She pulled off circling the blocks in the neighborhood a few times, finding no sign of Kay. Time was steadily ticking and she had to get back home. Kayla was trying her best to hold back tears as she drove away, but she had only a short time to get dressed and ready to go. She was so hurt, but crying wasn't going to change anything. This was her day of celebration and she swore to herself that she wasn't going to allow Kay to ruin it for her.

As soon as Kayla walked back in her door, the phone rang. There was the long lost Kay on the other end of the line. "Kayla where you at?" she asked like she had been waiting on her the whole time.

"I already came to pick you up and you weren't anywhere to be found," Kayla responded.

"I'm here now," Kay responded nonchalantly.

Kayla thought about getting smart with her mom and telling her about herself, but she didn't have time for the back and forth with her. Instead of wasting her breath and more time that she didn't have, she simply responded with, "I'll be there after I'm done getting dressed, Mom."

Kayla rushed to get ready and was now running behind schedule. Graduation started at 7, and she was supposed to be there by 6, but no later than 6:15, or she wouldn't be allowed to participate in the commencement ceremony. It was already after 5:00, and she couldn't risk what she worked so hard for. Kayla managed to get dressed and out of the house just a few minutes shy of six o' clock.

On the way out the door, Ray pulled up once again, got out the car, dressed all in black like he stepped off the cover of *GQ* magazine. With his black slacks and turtleneck, his black Stacy Adams, and this Italian gold rope chain with a cross. He was suited and booted for his baby girl's graduation. "Here you go," handing Kayla another card filled with money.

"Thank you Dad, I love you, but I have to go," she said. She wasn't trying to rush him off, but now she was just running late.

"Go on ahead I'll see you in a minute," he said. Ray just stood there smiling for a minute as the crew rode off. He was truly proud of Kayla. It had been a long road just like many of her other family members, and he too once doubted that she would cross that stage, but that day she had proven him wrong, and he couldn't have been happier.

Jackie, Keisha and Kayla headed out to pick up Kay so they could head to graduation. On the ride, Kayla was hoping and praying that Kay would be there and ready to go. As she pulled up to the house, Kay was there, but she definitely wasn't ready to go to anybody's graduation. Her mom was sitting on the porch holding a can of beer, wearing shorts, t-shirt, and flip flops, with her hair a mess all over her head. Kayla's mouth fell open in shock at her momma's appearance. She looked at Jackie and Keisha who were both speechless as well. Kayla jumped out of the car. "What are you doing?" Kayla yelled.

Kay gave her a look as if she wanted to say "What?"

"Why aren't you ready, Mom?"

"I thought I was getting ready at y'all house," Kay replied with the most serious look on her face.

"We were, but you weren't here when I came," Kayla screamed. That time she couldn't hold back her tears. Her mom was looking a complete mess and they didn't have time. "We don't have time for this shit," Kayla went on. She snatched the beer out of Kay's hands and poured it onto the concrete. "Fuck this shit!" Tears streamed down her face as she demanded Kay to get in the car.

Within seconds after pulling up and seeing her mom in that predicament, Kayla instantly flashed back to the many times her mom had let her down before. Those flashbacks fueled her anger. "This some stupid mothafuckin shit. How in the Fuck are you going to do this on my graduation day?" she asked. "Go to grandma, house" Kayla told Jackie as she continued to let Kay have it. "For years, you have put every single thing before me. I ask your ass for one damn day and this is the shit you do?" Kayla wasn't really asking Kay a question. It was rhetorical.

Kay got in the back seat and didn't say a word. Usually she'd try to fuck Kayla up for talking to her crazy, but she didn't have anything to say. Kayla cursed her out the whole ride to June's house.

When they pulled up, June and her Aunt Carla where coming down the stairs ready to attend Kayla's graduation. Kayla jumped out the car and ran up to her grandma and aunt and begged, "Please, please do something with her." They both looked at Kayla, and saw the desperation in her eyes and nodded.

"Get out," Kayla demanded. "They're going to try to get you ready, I have to go right now." Kay got out and Kayla sped off to the Civic Auditorium—it was now damn near 6:30. Kayla should have already been in her assigned seat. As soon as they pulled up on the grounds, Kayla jumped out.

"Bye, I love y'all," she screamed at Jackie and Keisha as she ran in her high-heels across the grass to get in to the auditorium.

"See you inside, we love you!" they yelled back in unison. Kayla was late, but she was still allowed to take her seat. She was the last graduate to arrive, and all of her classmates had already been seated. She didn't care; she was just happy she had made it. She pushed everything that just happened with her mom to the back of her mind so she could enjoy her moment.

As the ceremony began, she heard her family representing. "Kayla, Kayla, Kayla!" they chanted in unison . They seemed to have no regard for any rules or anyone else. They weren't alone in their cheers though, but it seemed like they were louder than anyone else's family in the auditorium. That was what graduation was about, so it was unrealistic for them to really think that anyone would be quiet until the ending.

～

When the principal and other school officials finally reached the letter T, and it was almost Kayla's turn to be called, she had a overwhelming sense of accomplishment. When they announced her name, she stood and walked across the stage to receive her high school diploma. A tear fell onto her cheek. Again, she heard her family loud and clear, cheering, howling, and rooting for her.

After the ceremony, the graduates walked out and Kayla heard someone screaming her name. "Kayla, Kayla, my baby!" She looked up and it was Kay screaming and leaning over the balcony. She even had tears running down her face. To Kayla's surprise, Kay was looking totally different from an hour ago. June and Carla had done a hell of a job getting Kay together. She had on a two-piece maroon skirt set, very little makeup, and her hair was combed. Of course, she had her signature rosy red cheeks. Kayla didn't know how they pulled it off; but they did, and still managed to make it to her graduation in time to see Kayla walk across the stage. This was definitely a night to remember.

In the hallway after the ceremony, they took several pictures. Kayla received congratulations and envelopes filled with cash from everyone. She truly felt like a star. They even convinced Ray to take a family picture with Kayla, and Kay. He was hesitant, but he did it for his daughter. He hated Kay with a passion, and she knew it. However, Kay saw this as an opportunity to get on everyone's good side. Just as the picture was about to be snapped, they both placed their arms around Kayla. Kay touched Ray's waist and he jumped and moved his hip all the way over just as the camera snapped at that exact moment. Another unforgettable moment to go down in history.

Finally, the longest/shortest day ever had come to an end. Kayla said goodbye, and expressed her appreciation to all those who came to support her. It was time to go and she was ready to celebrate.

"I'm going with y'all" Kay said, when Kayla asked her where she wanted to be dropped off.

"No you are not" Kayla quickly replied. She was through with her momma. Although, Kay made it to the graduation by the hair of her chinny chin chin, she made it and that's all Kayla wanted. Now it was time for her to go on about her business. "Well let me get a few dollars then", said Kay. She had the nerves to ask her daughter for any money. She should have been ashamed, but she wasn't at all. "That ain't going to happen" Kayla told her with an attitude. "You should be giving me some money, a gift or something. I'm the one that just graduated". Kay was trippen, it took them forever to get her up out of the vehicle. She really thought Kayla was going to give her some money. She ended up getting out of the car on the deuce four right in front of Evan's Towers, while Kayla, Jackie, and Keisha, left to go turn up. They went to their stomping grounds in Spencer Projects to Lisa's house. It was always a turn up over there, and if it wasn't one they would make it one.

— 1 —

ON THE RUN

Kayla so wished that she could go back in time, and take back everything that she said to the police the night before. If she only would have known that she was going to end up where she was at, she would have kept her mouth shut, but there was no turning back. She made her bed now it was time to lay in it. Usually she kept everything bottled up inside, but for whatever reason she finally told the truth about her situation. She finally let go of everything she had been holding inside for years. It felt good to let all that pain and hurt go, and tell the truth. She had been lying for years—to teachers, counselors, family, and her dad.

Kayla lied to everyone in an attempt to cover up Kay's wrongs in hopes that she would change like she had promised to do so many times. If she had known she would end up in a group home, she would have continued to hold her secrets inside. All the girls who stayed in the group home were either pregnant or had kids already. Kayla and her white roommate where the only exceptions, they didn't have any kids and weren't pregnant.

This was not where Kayla wanted to be, she wanted to be with her family. Her young mind couldn't process the idea that she was now actually in a better situation. She had been looking out for herself for quite a long time. Life wasn't perfect, but she was surviving. The police were not only doing their job, but looking out for her best interest and safety. They received a call stating that Kayla was a runaway and acted on their tip. They did what they were trained to do in that type of situation. She was not stable running the streets doing whatever she wanted. She was 12 years old, but she had been fending for herself for so long she thought that she was grown—or at least she felt like it.

The next morning after her arrival at the group home, Kayla barely ate breakfast. She hadn't been feeling too well lately, and she had no appetite at the moment. Then she met Paula, her new state case   worker who was given her case that morning. Paula introduced herself, and explained her role in Kayla's life. Kayla let the lady's words go into one ear and out of the other. Then she had to endure another orientation explaining what the C.A.R.E.S. program was about. All she heard was "blah, blah, blah". She didn't care to know anything that those people had to say to her. She didn't plan on being there long enough for any of it to matter any way.

For a few days she tried to play by the rules, by doing her chores and participating in the activities. However, not a minute went by that she wasn't planning an escape plan. She missed her life, her freedom, no matter how unstable it might have been.

Kayla and her roommate both discussed the possible ways they could escape, like leaving through the window in their room that led to the roof. The windows in the rooms were large enough for them to just walk on out, and they'd be on the roof. Another option was to just hop right on the elevators going to the first floor and walk straight out the door. Both of their plans were far-fetched and not well thought out. But, their desire to leave made them desperate. The jump from the roof didn't appear to be too high, but the landing was far enough up to be intimidating. So that plan of escape was a no go. Also by the time they got to the first floor on the elevator security would be notified and would catch them before they reached the front door. So far the escape plans where all unrealistic, all leading to dead ends.

Kayla spotted her first opportunity to run when one of the teen moms wanted to go outside to smoke a cigarette and asked Kayla to join her. The girl had decided she had been mentoring Kayla for the time she had been there, but in Kayla's eyes there wasn't a thing this girl could tell her. Kayla entertained her though, just to have someone to talk to. The girl had been looking out for her by giving her some of her hand-me-downs to wear since Kayla was brought in with nothing but the clothes on her back. The only thing that had stopped Kayla from running that day was the girl begging her not to run on her watch.

"I should just leave right now, my granny doesn't live far from here," Kayla mumbled to herself.

"No, please don't do that," the girl pleaded. "They are going to blame it on me because I asked if you could come outside with me."

Kayla thought I don't care, but she took the girl's statement into consideration and decided against making a run for it. "Well let me hit that cigarette then," Kayla requested sort of as a bargaining tool. They shared the cigarette and went back inside the building.

Kayla had been at the group home for about a week. She hadn't talked to her mom, dad, or anyone in her family.

The people at the group home did get ahold of Ray's sister Michelle who gave them the last information she knew about Kay, but that led them nowhere. Kayla was unaware of the authorities unsuccessful attempts to convince Michelle to keep and look after Kayla until Kay became reachable. Michelle had tried to intervene once before with Kayla, and it didn't work out. She didn't want to deal with the stress of raising a teenage girl. Not one person that they contacted that first night was willing to take her in.

The police tried contacting Kay the night they originally picked Kayla up, but they had been unsuccessful. Then after Kayla opened up about her situation and living environment, being returned to Kay wasn't an option.

A few days later, the center planned to take the girls to a movie at the Dollar Movie Theatre in South Omaha. They went to go see the sixth man. Kayla had been actually anticipating seeing that movie with Marlon Wayans and Dwayne Wayne from *A Different World*. However, her desire to escape was stronger than her want to see that movie. She figured she'd see that movie at another time. Kayla decided this was her opportunity—she was getting out that day. So as the girls found their seats, Kayla made it a point to sit near the back.

"Come sit up here with us," the others said, noticing Kayla sitting off by herself.

"No, I'm fine. I like sitting in the back," she responded.

The chaperon started to say something else, but hesitated and said, "Okay," as she sat down with the other girls towards the front of the theatre.

As soon as the lights in the theatre dimmed and the opening credits started to play, Kayla exited the theater. She didn't really have a game plan—she just knew she was leaving right then and there. She walked to the Hy-Vee grocery store. She knew she didn't have much time before they realized that she was missing. She called her granny and convinced her to give her a few dollars. Her granny was headed out on her weekly trip garage sale exploring, and had no idea what was going on with her granddaughter. So without question she agreed to leave the money in the mail box. She just said "okay, baby, I'll leave the money in the mailbox. Now Kayla's only issue was that she had to figure out how she was going to get from south Omaha to north Omaha. She would have been better off running from the center which was already North. She didn't consider any of that prior to running, it was a spur-of-the-moment decision. At that moment she spotted an older African American couple about ready to leave the grocery store. She hesitantly approached them to ask for a ride, and quickly made up a story about being left behind at the show. The couple didn't question her story at all, and agreed to give her a ride.

Once she arrived at her granny's house off of 39th and Burdette Street she opened the mailbox and grabbed a folded piece of notebook paper containing the $15. Then she took off on foot the 30 to 45 minutes back to Anne's house on Florence Boulevard where she had been staying before she got picked up.

"Hey," Anne and her kids were shocked to see Kayla. They didn't have a clue as to what had happened or what was going on with Kayla after the cops drove off with her in the back of the police car. "What's going on? Where you been?" they asked. The last time they saw Kayla, she was being forced into the back of the cop's car about a week prior. Kayla explained her whereabouts and what had happened during the time she was gone. Although Anne had a large family of her own, she wasn't going to allow Kayla to just be out on the streets on her own. Anne told Kayla she could stay.

Kayla wore the same size clothing as Anne's oldest daughter, Shamika. Shamika took a liking to Kayla just like a little sister. So she made sure she had a change of clean clothes. Plus, she had left some underwear, shoes, and a few clothing items from her prior stay.. Kayla was happy to be back in familiar territory. Anne's was a kick it spot, as long as the kids kept her house clean she really didn't care what they did. It was a party every day. The house was always filled with guests and overnight visitors. That was right up Kayla's alley. Kayla was already fast in the ass, so living with minimal to no supervision was not good for her. But it was the ideal place for a teenager who wanted to hang out and party.

During the time she had been hanging at Anne's house she had a few sexual encounters. CP, short for Chocolate Playa, was a hood dude who hung out in New Jack City, some apartments on 16th street. The apartments were called "New Jack City" because they reminded people of the apartment complex on the movie New Jack City. They were run down, low-income housing, that had a high crime rate.

He was this young chocolate boy who wasn't doing too bad for his age. All the neighborhood girls were attracted to him. Kayla was no exception she always eyed him whenever she seen him, and one day he spoke to her after noticing her staring him down.

"Hey lil mama, what's up with you?" he asked. From then on out she made a point to talk to him. Only issue was that Anne's stepdaughter used to date him. So he was supposed to be off limits. Off limits or not Kayla continued to talk to CP and eventually they hooked up, but once they hooked up he was no longer interested. He was young and fine and had way too many options to just give his attention to one female. Then there was this young cat nicknamed Stutter Blood who came by Anne's house on a daily basis. He was cute also. Kayla really didn't have any interest in him, but one night while she was asleep on the couch. He woke her up and started touching on her. One thing led to the next and she had sex with him right there on the couch while everyone was asleep.

After she left the theatre that night, almost a whole week went by before anyone came looking for Kayla. Or at least until they found where she was hiding out. One early morning, Kayla's caseworker from the C.A.R.E.S. program showed up at Anne's door. Kayla was ready to run again if need be, she didn't want to return to the Salvation Army C.A.R.E.S. program at all. After talking to Anne and Kayla, the caseworker was going to submit a request for Kayla to be temporarily placed in Anne's home legally. In the meantime, she had given Anne a voucher for Kayla to get a few clothing and personal items she had been without since she'd been on the run.

The caseworker's plan did not go as Kayla expected. Anne's family was already large, there was not enough room for Kayla, and it turned out that Anne had some prior involvement with Child Protective Services herself. The caseworker returned with the bad news, and had received instructions to remove Kayla from Anne's home. In addition to Anne not meeting the qualifications required by state law to house Kayla, Kay had given her input as well. Anne use to stay with her niece, and from what she had heard, Anne wasn't too stable. Although Kay was running the streets doing drugs, she didn't believe that Kayla should be staying at Anne's either. Kay was right about Anne to be concerned, but she had the nerve to do it. However, it didn't matter either way because Kayla wasn't going to be placed there.

Kayla took off out the side door without her shoes or any of her belongings. Anne sent her nephew after Kayla who had to physically pick her up and carry her back. Even if she couldn't look after her, she didn't want her out on the streets. Kayla was devastated that she could not stay, and she did not want to go anywhere with that caseworker. It took almost an hour for Anne to calm her down and convince her to leave with the lady.

— 2 —

I'M NOT CRAZY

Kayla went from Anne's to The Y.E.S. (Youth Emergency Services) House located near St. Joseph hospital off Cuming Street. Kayla didn't want to stay there either, but at that point she didn't have a choice. She made herself sick with all the fighting and crying she did before she finally gave in. Once her caseworker made sure she was settled in, she left Kayla there in her new temporary placement. Kayla took a seat off in the corner by herself, and didn't mumble a word to a soul. The girls attempted to talk to her, but she gave them nothing but mean looks. If looks could kill that whole entire house would be deceased.

Suddenly Kayla started dry-heaving and throwing up. She hadn't had much in her stomach so the only things coming up were saliva and bile. Her belly was cramping something serious, and the pain was unbearable. One of the staff came over to check on her, and decided that taking her to the hospital would be the best choice.

Once arriving at the hospital it seemed like forever before the doctor saw Kayla. After a few tests, they discovered that she was pregnant and having a miscarriage. Kayla was in pain, scared, and emotional upon hearing the news. After getting the necessary procedures, she sat in the room alone until the hospital psychologist came in with some procedural questions for her. After the psych evaluation they determined that Kayla was suicidal. They came to that conclusion because she stated that she wanted to "kill herself" and her unwillingness to interact with them. Hours went by and Kayla remained in that room by herself crying. She wasn't crying because she had lost a baby she didn't even know she was pregnant with; she was crying because she was in a situation that she had no control over. Aside from the pain she physically felt, the miscarriage didn't mean much to her. She was sure it was this guy JD's baby. She had had a few sexual encounters with him that summer. He was the only one she had unprotected sex with, but she didn't plan on telling him or anyone else, for that matter. Due to her circumstances, the medical staff had no one to notify, so that incident was one that stayed between them and Kayla. Crazy as it sounds even if they did have someone to notify. It was Kayla's decision to disclose the information. They brought her a sandwich, chips, and juice, but she barely touched it. She just laid there in silence in a daze consumed by her thoughts.

Kayla would never forget the first time that she met JD. JD was 15 or 16 years old, caramel colored skin, long hair that he kept in a ponytail to the back. He was the only Blood that hung out in the projects, but everyone was cool about it. He had what they liked to call a hood pass. It was the first night she hung out with Mo Mo. Mo Mo introduced her as his new chicken head. Kayla wasn't mature enough or didn't have the street knowledge to know that it was an insult.

JD was sure checking her out, she was a new face. He hadn't seen her around in the projects before. Although, Kayla's family had been living down in Spencer for years. Kayla had been around, but wasn't no one checking for her walking around with ponytails and ball balls in her hair.

She had grown up a little—she now had some hips and ass, and some titties to look at. The project niggas started to notice her.

JD was originally stopped in his tracks before he could say a word to Kayla. However, that didn't stop him from checking for her. Considering Mo Mo had a girlfriend, Cynthia, he only entertained Kayla during his free time. Kayla quickly got jealous. Being young she figured she'd get some attention elsewhere. JD happened to be around so she started showing him interest. It helped that he was fine.

It didn't take long to get his attention, she knew he was interested already from their first encounter. Men (in his case, boys) were easily distracted by looks, and she had those. She started off with a little flirting, by playing the staring game. She noticed he kept up with his shoe game, so she used that to spark a conversation. Soon, they were a secret thing.

Kayla liked JD, but Mo Mo had her mind occupied. Whenever he felt like coming around, Kayla would drop whatever or whoever, and welcome him with open arms. She thought she loved that man, and nothing he could do or say to change the fact. JD had her lusting as well because she'd jump for him when he came around too. Fats had told her that this is exactly where she would end up, being passed back and forth between the homies, but she let what he said go in one ear and out of the other.

A few hours passed, and Kayla had no clue what was going on. Finally a nurse entered and told her that her ride was there. Still unaware of what was happening Kayla grab her belongings and prepared to leave.

Outside was a small white vehicle that looked like a mix between a van and a small SUV. Something like she had seen in the movies. Kayla got in and she quickly realized that she wasn't headed back to the YES house. The YES house was across the street a few blocks from the hospital. After 10-15 minutes Kayla noticed the street sign that said "Dorcas Street," as they pulled up to a large building the looked like a hospital. Once the vehicle stopped a few minutes later, a man and two women came out of the hospital doors and walked towards the van. Kayla refused to get out the vehicle on her own. So they had to force her. They grabbed her as she pulled away, kicking and screaming. Kayla fought hard even though she was in pain from just miscarrying, but she was no competition for these three people. They were very familiar with cases like this and had done this many times before. After a moment, they easily gained control of the situation. Once inside, Kayla still refused to calm down and follow instructions. So they were forced to put her in a strait jacket and lock her in a padded room. Kayla had only seen places like this on television. She now realized that it wasn't just make believe on TV—this type of place really existed. She tried to put up a fight for a while longer, but now restrained in a padded room she realized that it was useless.

Finally she sat down and waited for someone to come back into the room. She was being observed through a two-way mirror, so once they could visibly see that she had calmed down they re-entered the room. "Are you going to cooperate now?" the nurse asked her. Kayla nodded yes, she was still unwilling to talk to them. She did not want to be there, nor did she want to understand why she was there in the first place.

A psychological evaluation at St Joseph Mental Hospital was 72 hours/3 days. Each day that Kayla had to go to sleep and wake up in that place was a nightmare to her. It seemed like an eternity and she felt like she would never get out.

The kids in there really had some issues, she thought. Kayla's life wasn't peaches and cream, but she was nothing like the kids she was surrounded with. Some of the kids were suicidal for real. One girl she attended group counseling with had jumped out of a moving vehicle as her mom drove on the interstate, and she had the scars to show for it. Another boy was a problem child major anger issues and beat up on his siblings and his mom on a daily. When Kayla told the doctors and nurses that she wanted to kill herself, she was being sarcastic and not serious at all. But whether she was serious or not they had to do their job, and that is how she ended up in the crazy hospital for 72 hours. At that point, there was nothing that she could do or say that would get her out of this situation before her evaluation was completed.

That first night she just went to her room and cried in pain until she finally fell asleep. The next day she stayed mute and refused to talk to anybody. She was deep in thought she had just lost her unborn child. She didn't know how to feel about it, she was young and wasn't ready for a baby, but at the same time she felt empty, and she was grieving the loss of her baby. She ate her meals she went to group counseling, but she said not a word to anyone, except for asking the staff for permission to use the telephone.

For the first time in months she talked to her mom, Kay. At that point, Kay couldn't do much for her daughter either. However they did allow her to come up for a visit which made Kayla feel better. After visiting with her mom, Kayla opened up just a little bit more, but not too much. She was always taught to keep her business to herself, and that family business was just that—family business—so it was hard for her to veer from what she had always known and followed her whole life. Each counseling session was the same, everyone would talk and when was Kayla's turn, she'd say, "I don't want to kill myself, I was just angry." She wasn't lying; she didn't want to kill herself. She did have problems and issues in her life, but she wasn't about to tell a room full of strangers. She was still holding on to the saying that family business is family business. She could not see how opening up to these people would help her so she didn't. She wasn't going to say, "My momma is a crackhead, my daddy don't have the time, I just had a miscarriage." None of that was their business, it was hers; and as far as she was concerned it would stay that way.

Everything about that place sucked except for the food. Every meal was like a buffet and for dinner patients went down to the cafeteria. They could eat as much as they wanted—there were no limits whatsoever. On day two, Kayla was shocked to see her cousin Netta in the cafeteria; they were holding her on a different floor. They tried to speak to one another but that was not allowed at all. Once a staff observed them attempting to converse, it was stopped immediately. Kayla didn't know why they made such a big deal about it. The staff explained that they were not allowed to converse due to being on different levels which was some sort of rule.

Over the next few days, Kayla relaxed a little bit from the way she was the first night. Not a moment passed that she wasn't trying to get up and out of that place. It was definitely not for her. All day there was one-on-one counseling and group counseling. All day it was a repeat of the same stuff. Kayla felt that she had absolutely nothing at all in common with the others who were there.

"Can I call my mom?" she asked a staff member, and turned around just as her Aunt Anne stepped off the elevator. She was confused to see her aunt there.

"You ready to go?" Anne asked, and Kayla answered "Yes!" super excited. She ran to her room to gather her things. She no longer cared about making that phone call to her mom, she just wanted to go.

Kayla was going to stay with her aunt Anne. She didn't care where she was going or how she was getting there at that point, as long as she was getting out of that crazy hospital.

Apparently, Kay had asked Anne to take Kayla in as a favor, and Anne agreed. Once Anne said yes, Kay left town to start a new life in Minnesota with her boyfriend Lewis. She didn't bother to tell her daughter goodbye; she just disappeared. Kay didn't stop, pass GO or collect two-hundred dollars. She just hit the highway with Lewis and was gone with the wind. Kay had once again abandoned her daughter. Kayla hated her mother for being selfish, and leaving her. She should have been Kay's first priority, but like many times before she showed her daughter that she was not. Kayla came second to drugs, and now she was even coming in second after her man. Kayla suppressed her thoughts and decided to be happy with the right now. She was out of that crazy hospital and that was all she wanted at the moment.

Things were different at Anne's house from when Kayla was a child. The young girl used to love to spend time at her aunt's house. Anne always had the best activities for them to do, flash cards, bingo, Monopoly. She took the kids on outings to the movies, magic shows, whatever there was to do in the community Anne knew about it and took her kids, and Kayla often was able to tag along.

However, as an older pre-teen those activities and outings were a bore to Kayla. She wasn't that innocent little girl she once used to be. She had been exposed to grown up shit and that's what entertained her and had her interest. Anne still wanted to take them on outings to air shows, museums, and to the library and things of that nature. That was only fun for her and her daughter who was still young.

Kayla had been staying with her aunt Anne for nearly two months when everything started to go sour. Anne had a whole different set of rules in her household that Kayla was not used to at all. Anne would wake up one day and decide that there would be no TV for the day, She'd say, "read a book," when the kids asked what they should do. Kayla huffed, yeah read a book she thought. Kayla was miserable staying with her aunt 90 percent of the time.

Anne even put her niece Kayla on a punishment until she got on some type of birth control. Anne knew that her niece was sexually active, so she decided to do some preventive care. Soon after her arrival, Anne scheduled a pelvic exam and pap smear for her niece. Kayla understood that she needed to be on some form of birth control after her incident. However, Anne knew nothing of that situation—she was just doing what needed to be done. She would have done the same thing for her daughter. Kayla was still a child herself, and in her predicament she was unable to care for herself, let alone a baby.

That appointment would be one to remember. First mistake the doctor made was to allow his student doctors to sit in on the exam. This wasn't Kayla's first exam. In fact she had just had one after her miscarriage. Kayla was afraid that this exam would reveal her secret. When, the doctor inserted that cold metal tool into her vagina, and that was it—she lost it. She was still tender and uncomfortable from her recent D and C procedure.

She demanded to them to stop. They ignored her request and continued with the procedure, but Kayla flipped quickly.

"Get the fuckoff of me, and leave me alone," she said.

Everyone in the room stood in shock in awkward silence—the doctor, the student doctors, and her aunt Anne. Then Kayla commanded that everyone get out of the room, and they complied. Anne was still speechless—she said absolutely nothing to her niece when the room was cleared. A few minutes later the doctor returned, and tried to talk to Kayla. However, Kayla had completely shut down. She was unwilling to listen—she just wanted to get out of there.

They left the office, but Anne made it clear that Kayla was on a punishment until she got on some sort of birth control. Kayla couldn't care less what her aunt was talking about, but she wasn't about to go through that procedure again. Kayla complained that it was painful, but Anne didn't understand how it hurt because Kayla was already sexually active. Eventually, Anne learned that Kayla was uncomfortable with all the extra people (student doctors) in the room.

Anne said, "I understand that. I get it. But we'll still have to go back to the doctor. We just won't let them bring others in to the room."

Kayla agreed to go back and complete the exam and to get on birth control. However Anne played zero games. Kayla would remain on punishment until the appointment was completed. Anne also had a trick up her sleeve, she preferred the depo-vera shot for Kayla rather than the pill that she agreed to take. She bribed her niece with a dress from a new fashion store on North 30th Street—Joe's Fashion. They had recently opened their doors, and they carried a line of long floral body dresses that Kayla liked and that where very popular at the time. Anne had already bought her one, but she promised another if Kayla agreed to get the shot. Kayla agreed just like that; she liked clothes, so this was right up her alley.

Kayla had grown used to living a life with limited rules and barely any direction. Anne had a list of rules and expectations that Kayla had a hard time adjusting to. Anne refused to let the kids just sit around each day and do nothing constructive. So she signed her son Twan and Kayla up for the Sun Dawgs summer program. Twan was already 13 and Kayla was a pre-teen. They both objected to going to the program, but they had no other choice at that point.

Twan and Kayla were the oldest kids in the program, which made it awkward for them. Anne did not care, she still made them go daily. They would sit on the picnic tables at Kountze Park and converse with each other most of the day. They didn't interact with the other kids or participate in any activities except for lunch. They actually had more in common with the staff who weren't that much older. The staff sympathized with Twan and Kayla; they understood why they didn't like coming to the program and participating. After a few weeks of Sun Dawgs torture, they started walking to their grandmother June's house every day, then eventually Twan made his way to his friend Will's house, and Kayla started hanging out with her older cousins Avery and Jackie. Anne wasn't happy with Kayla hanging with her older cousins, but she decided to go ahead and allow her niece to hang out and not go to Sun Dawgs anymore. Kayla was happy; she would be willing to do anything if it meant she could avoid going to kiddie camp all day.

Avery and Jackie were way more fun to hang with. They all formed a clique they called ABC short for All Bitches Club. Avery was TNB (top notch bitch), Jackie was (looney bitch), Kayla was (crazy bitch), Avery's friend Trina was (big bitch) and Kesha was (baby bitch). All of them together were a hot mess. They did a lot of random, daring, and dumb shit. Together they stole, started trouble with people, and more. To them it was all fun and games, especially to the youngest of the crew, Kayla and Kesha. Kayla and Kesha got initiated in the crew, they don't know what exactly they did, but they did so much crazy stuff they were in, and that was good enough for them. They were the youngest in the crew, but the feistiness for sure. That summer would be one to remember.

Hanging with Avery, Jackie, and their friends was everything to Kayla. It was like a whole new life. Avery had a car, and she transported them everywhere they went. Notorious B.I.G. was popular at the time. So they'd ride around listening to his music quoting the verses word for word.

After only a few months of Kayla staying with her Aunt Anne, she was done and over the situation. In that short amount of time, Kayla had overstayed her welcome. Kayla had no chance against her aunt's rules. Anne's daughter Alexis couldn't do any wrong in Anne's eyes, but the truth was she was one annoying child. She was aggravating. However, Anne had her blinders on when it came to her baby girl.

Kayla and Anne went to church one Sunday with their aunt Lynn, and Alexis sat next to Kayla bothering her during the whole service long. Kayla moved away from her little cousin, and then didn't talk to her for the remainder of the service.

Kayla went back to her Aunt Lynn's house and Alexis went home with Anne. A few hours later, Anne called Lynn's house.

"Hello" Kayla said getting on the phone with her aunt.

"You hit Alexis today at church?" she asked Kayla with an aggravated tone.

"No" Kayla responded, confused about her aunt's question.

"Well Alexis said you hit her at church today."

"No I didn't," Kayla responded with an attitude. Anne didn't believe Kayla she had already concluded that Kayla hit her daughter before she even asked.

"Well you coming home tomorrow, because you don't be putting your hands on nobody," Anne demanded. Kayla hung up the phone, pissed off about the lie her little cousin had made up. Immediately the phone rang again, "Hello." Kayla answered.

"Why you hang up in my face" Anne asked on the other line.

"I didn't" Kayla responded, still angry.

"Well next time you say bye," Anne insisted, but Kayla ended the call again without saying bye. After that, Anne decided that she was done with her niece. Kayla hanging up in her face was a sign of disrespect and there was no way that she was going to allow her niece to be disrespectful towards her. Anne didn't waste any time moving her niece out of her house. The next day she packed all Kayla's belongings and delivered them to her at Lynn's house.

— 3 —

IN MY PROJECTS

"Let's go smoke a blunt with the homie Slim," Michael said to Kayla, Quila, and Fats as they sat on the stoop talking and chilling. So they walked across the street to the assisted living units and went to the back. A tall skinny dark skin dude came to the door.

"What up," they said as they embraced each other with a high five and a half hug.

"We came to get you high since you can't come out of the house," Slim laughed and came out the door to the porch. Kayla noticed his ankle bracelet and realized he was on house arrest.

He looked at her and asked, "Who is this," as he looked her up and down. He had never seen her before. Kayla looked him up and down right back.

"This all me, my nigga," Michael replied taking claim on the young girl interrupting the staring contest the both were having. After they smoked a couple of blunts, they left. Kayla walked off with Quila.

"Girl, Slim is fine" she said. For a moment Michael was an after thought. The only thing on her mind was the fine dark chocolate nigga she just met.

Soon Slim was off house arrest, and he had become a main face that was seen in the projects every day. His hustle game was strong. Not too long after he was released off house arrest, he was in a new whip. He had the average box Chevy that most of the niggas had, but he had it sitting pretty on some rims and a fresh paint job, with some nice beats.

Michael had been acting "sometimey" going back and forth. One minute he was fucking with Kayla, and the next minute he was proclaiming how she was too young. So she started to show interest in other niggas besides him. She had had her eyes on Slim since the day she first met him. Kayla easily lured Slim in with her flirting and next thing you knew they were a thing. Kayla didn't try to hide it she'd be right up on him in Michael's face. Michael noticed, but the playa in him made him act as if he didn't care.

"Fuck you, muthafucka. I'm gonna fuck you up," Shaun was screaming at Mike as he rode his ten-speed mountain bike down the street laughing at her. Shaun was pissed at Mike for some reason. No one knew what he had done, but they knew that he had Shaun fucked up. She was outside in her what used to be white bra that was a couple of sizes too small showing all her stretch marks and everything. She didn't have any shame what so ever. She was showing her ass that day putting on a whole show for whoever was outside to see. Mike kept riding in circles and taking off whenever she got close just antagonizing her and making her more pissed off than she already was. That was one of the first times Kayla had seen her show her ass and act a fool behind a nigga, but it definitely wouldn't be her last.

～

Rico was a little short cutie who started hanging in the projects. Keisha had her eyes on him from the first time she had seen him. Rico had long natural curly hair, he had the perfect chocolate complexion, and he was always clean. He had the best of everything. It was evident that he was good and taken care of.

He really didn't fit in at all in the projects. He was down there every day hanging out with the niggas, smoking, drinking, he even called himself hustling. He didn't need to do that but he wanted to fit in and be hood. Rico had a slick mouth though. He was always being disrespectful toward the girls in the projects. That's how he and Keisha ended up falling off due to his mouth. He may have gotten away with the disrespect with most of the females, but when it came to Kayla and Keisha, he had them messed up. They would go toe for toe, word for word with his ass. It had gotten to the point where they were ready to fight him.

"Shut up you bitches," Rico said as he came up on their porch one day out of the clear blue sky. He didn't realize he had fucked up. After those words escaped his mouth. The girls let him have it.

"Fuck you, you short bitch ass nigga. We will fuck you up!"

"Do it then."

They passed words back and forth for a quick minute. Then Kayla and Keisha stormed in the house. They needed to change clothes. The both of them had on dresses. Lynn and Jackie were playing a game and didn't notice them come in, but as they were headed back outside they noticed.

"Why y'all change clothes, what's going on?"

"Because Rico about to get his ass beat."

The girls were so mad they didn't care about cussing in front of Lynn. Lynn and Jackie put the game on pause and followed the girls outside. They first tried to calm the situation down, but Rico and that mouth kept going. He got to calling Jackie and Lynn some bitches too Next thing you knew Jackie had punched him dead in the mouth. That didn't shut his ass up though he kept going. At that point that's when a few of the niggas from the projects intervened and snatched his little ass up and got him out of the way.

The feud didn't end there. A few days later they were all down at Lisa's house kicking it as usual. Then Fat's came over with Rico tagging right behind him. It was still filled with animosity from a few days ago, so words quickly transpired between him and the girls.

"You ready?" Kayla said looking at Keisha giving her the cue to get ready to fuck his ass up.

"Yup!" she replied. Then she pushed Rico. Rico quickly rushed her, that's when Kayla came around the couch and started punching him. The girls both were hitting him left and right. Somehow they went from the middle of the living room over to the stairs. Kayla was sitting on the stairs while Rico was in the middle in between her legs constantly getting hit, and Keisha was hovering over him at the bottom of the stairs hitting him.

"Stop it y'all, stop!" Lisa yelled from the top of the stairs. She had been in her room getting dressed and ready to go out. She heard all the commotion and came out of her room to see them fighting their asses off in her house. That's when Fat's attempted to break it up, getting hit in the process. Finally he was able to separate them but he had a hard time keeping Kayla and Keisha back.

"I told your ass to leave them girls alone." Fat's told Rico while laughing at him. They still wanted to fight. Rico already had scratches galore and blood dripping from his face, but that wasn't enough. He had been asking for that ass whooping. Lisa had to run a few doors down to get Lynn to come help break things up. They were fighting so hard Rico came up out of his shoe. So Kayla grabbed his Jordan and ran across the street throwing it in the field. As Lynn was coming, Rico somehow got loose and cold cocked Keisha right in her eye. Lynn quickly rushed him and slammed him up against the project wall. Kayla came around her aunt, and got a few more good hits in.

$\sim$

The ABC crew used to just like to have fun. They'd do crazy shit from going on jacking sprees. To goofy shit like riding through the projects on top of the car.

On one of their riding through the jets on top of the car days, they heard some females yell, "Y'all need to get y'all dumb asses off that car." Avery stopped at first ready to say something back. Instead they ignored the girls and kept on going. The next day they saw the same females that lived in the back.

"There go those bitches that was talking shit yesterday," Keisha said loud enough for them to hear her. Next thing you know they started talking shit and the argument started. Inky and Big Momma were known for jumping on folks and pulling out knives and cutting people with no problem. So Jackie, Avery, Keisha, and Kayla made sure they were very observant. Inky came around to the front with her crew, and kept talking shit with her hand in her purse.

"Bitch, ain't nobody scared of no knife. You're gonna have to get to it first," Jackie said as she was walking up on Inky daring her to make a move. Lynn came outside and attempted to defuse the situation which succeeded. Inky and her crew went back to their area in the back and that was the end of that. A few hours later after everything died down. Inky came knocking on Lynn's door.

"I just want to apologize to you and your daughters. I don't want any problems. I was wrong and shouldn't have come to y'all like that." She had a change of heart she no longer wanted to fight or cause any problems. She realized they all had to live around each other and didn't want to be walking around watching her back on a daily. Lynn had a reputation in Spencer. Everyone knew that she was not to be fucked with. She may have been getting older, but she still would go there if need be. Even so, they agreed not to fight Inky and her crew. They only backed down out of respect for their mom and aunt.

That wasn't the only time one of the chicks from the projects tried to fight one of the Thompson girls. There was this high yellow chick they called White Cheese as a nickname. She was actually friends with Renay and had stayed with her for a while when she lived off 16th and Victor Street. Couldn't nobody tell White Cheese that she wasn't cute. Wasn't anything special about her looks. She was your average red bone chick. She thought she was the finest thing walking the projects. She also had an arrogant attitude, and thought that everyone was beneath her. She talked so much shit she thought people were scared of her because no one never really challenged her. That didn't do anything but boost her ego, but she just hadn't come across the right person. Until she thought she was gonna come at Avery sideways.

Avery was a bigger girl and was comfortable in her skin. She was very confident and she had been big her whole life so she had heard all of the fat jokes a person could imagine. She and White Cheese got into over a small understanding, but White Cheese refused to drop the issue and just let it go. She made it a point to talk shit to and about Avery to anyone that would listen. Usually Avery wasn't one for confrontation. She wasn't scared; she just really wasn't the fighting type. For weeks the insults and trash talking kept coming her way from Tinese. Finally Lynn got tired of it.

"Come on Avery, you about to shut her ass up," Lynn said as she grabbed her niece by the arm and walked her across the street to fight the girl. Tinese didn't really want to fight.

As Avery approached her she kept running her mouth "Fat bitch this, fat bitch that." That's when Avery showed her what a fat bitch could do. She swung on the girl and she flew back onto the porch. Avery then hovered over her giving her several more punches to the body. White Cheese tried to fight back but she just wasn't a match for Avery. Avery was beating her up so badly that she just stopped. No one else was trying to break it up. White Cheese's cousin Worm was on the side line screaming, "That's my cousin, that's my cousin," but she knew not to jump in. Lynn and Jackie were waiting on her to try it so they could whoop off in her ass too.

After getting her ass beat she had nothing more to say. Her high yellow complexion was covered with bruises from the beating she had just taken. After that day White Cheese didn't show her face too much down in the projects. She had been embarrassed. Her mouth had finally gotten her into some shit she couldn't get out of. Just like any other fight, it was talked about for a few days but as soon as the next thing happened, everyone forgot about it and moved on.

There was never a dull moment in the projects. From Mr. Mitchell ,the OHA site manager for the Spencer property. Stayed on the job, he'd be up and at it at 5 am, citing every resident he could for not maintaining the cleanliness in front of their units. When he was busy citing folks and issuing fines. He was patrolling for the band and bard. Mr. Mitchell wasn't one to play, it was his mission to keep the projects up to par, even if that meant that he wasn't well liked. But then, he didn't get paid to be liked. He was a one-man army, and the moment his presence was gone all the undesirable activities resumed.

Most days, there wasn't much to do in the projects. Kayla and her cousin mostly hung out sitting on the stoop as they watched everything that went on. They were among the first to know when anything went down. One day they witnessed the whole 29th Street block get surprise raided by the gang unit. The gang unit knew who everyone was already and always hoped that they'd catch a few young boys slipping. One dude called "D" always lucked up and got away. Either it was pure luck or the fact that he was always alert and aware of his surroundings. He was ready to disappear at the sight of police, a drive by, or anything else coming his way. Living the street life, we had to stay ready at all times for whatever came our way.

On any given day, we could be sure there would be some surprise action of some sort. From an argument to a full-blown fight. On one pretty normal day, the girls decided to take a walk down 30th Street. On the walk back down 30th near Manderson Street, they decided to stop at the newly-opened corner store. Out of all the things it could have been named, it was named the "Butt Hutt." The store didn't even look open, the door was closed, and the blinds were down. They still walked up on the porch and started to peek through the window to see what the inside looked like. Instead, they got an eye-full.

A man and woman were butt-ass naked, getting it in on the love seat that sat in the middle of the floor. All you could see was his ass, pounding her up and down and her legs wildly swinging in the air.

"No wonder they closed," Avery joked, and the girls burst into laughter. The man must have heard them because he jumped up so fast. All you could see was balls swinging. The girls backed up and waited for him to come to the door, and he did. He came to the door with nothing but his pants on—no shirt, drawers or nothing. Just his pants.

"Can I help you'" he said as if this wasn't a store. The man was obviously embarrassed, and had very little to say. He let them into the story, and the woman who was just spread eagle on the couch was nowhere to be seen. The few minutes inside the store were awkward. They left, but joked about that for days. The store had truly lived up to its name!

Another time while they hung out on the stoop, they watched one of the neighborhood dudes named Chuck hit the corner. In the next five minutes he came back around that corner, but he was all beat up and bloody. We later found out that he had just tried to jack a crackhead. That move backfired on him—he had the wrong crackhead that day, and had underestimated the strength of the addict. He was no match against that man's will and determination to get high that day.

That's just how it was in the Spencer—it was either boring or all the way live Channel 7 Action News.

— 4 —
LOVE LOST

Kayla stayed at Lynn's for a few weeks. It was Summer time so Lynn really didn't mind. From there, Kayla went to stay with her dad and granny around the time school was starting back. After that she went to go live with Ray and her granny. Ray was barely at home, so it was more like Kayla was living with her granny. At the time, her cousin was staying there with her two kids and was pregnant. She had been staying with her granny due to her kid's father getting her house shot up; she was scared to be at her own home. The house was crowded, but they all managed to live there together.

Ray had a girlfriend that he spent most of his time with. He'd come to the house to check on his daughter and take her to school, but outside of that he wasn't there too often. Kayla had become friends with a girl, Dee, who stayed a few houses up the block and they hung out on a regular. Both of the girls were entering high school as freshman and attended Central. When Ray didn't give Kayla a ride to school, the two girls rode the city bus together.

On the weekends Kayla would go to spend the night at her aunt Lynn's, which she liked. She got to be down in the projects being hot in the ass. She got to see Michael who she thought she was in love with. He may have been too old for her, but she didn't care. Her age didn't stop him from showing interest. They'd make out all the time and he always smoked weed with her, so she was happy.

Kayla only had eyes for Michael until she met Sidney—he was called Sid for short. One day walking home from the bus stop from school, Kayla and Dee had gotten off the bus at Andy's and Lillie's to buy some snacks. On their way home they ran into Sid and his friend. Kayla had actually known Sid since they were kids going to Smith Temple Church. Back then he was a little ugly black kid that got on her nerves, always bothering people. Also her aunt Lynn had married his late uncle Bernard who had passed a few years prior. Sid wasn't that little black annoying little kid anymore though. He had grown up into a handsome young man.

"Hey, what's your name?" he said to Kayla before she and Dee could walk by. Kayla looked at Dee, who said, "Don't look at me, he talking to you."

Kayla said, "Hey" back all shy. She didn't immediately make a connection to who he was.

"Come here," he said, motioning her to come to him. So Kayla walked towards him.

"Damn you look good," he said. Kayla had on some brown flare pants and a midriff shirt that matched. They talked for a few minutes and exchanged numbers.

"Be safe," he said, as they continued on. Kayla was blushing for the remainder of the walk home. Every day after that Kayla made it a point to get off the number 35 bus and walk past Sid's house. They talked on the phone all the time. He constantly tried to get Kayla to sneak out and come over. She sure wanted to but she couldn't get away that easy on school days. Ray stayed on her neck about everything that she did, especially since it hadn't been that long ago since she snuck boys into her granny's house and scared the living shit out of granny and then tried to lie and say the boys were her cousins.

Every weekend Kayla made her way back down to the projects to her Aunt Lynn's house or up to Pleasant View at Shaun's house. Between those two places there was always some trouble to get into. Kayla never was ready to go back home after hanging out drinking, smoking, and being grown all weekend. Ray threatened time and time again that he wouldn't allow her to go back if she wasn't ready to go when it was time to go. Kayla constantly ignored him.

She was still talking to Sid on the phone every day, he finally convinced her to skip school to come and chill with him all day. It was on a Thursday, Kayla got up that morning like she usually did. She made sure she took another shower even though she took one the night before; she put lotion every inch of her body. She put on one of her long floral body dresses her aunt Anne had brought her over the summer; flat ironed her hair and everything. She was looking cute when she walked out the door for "school." She walked to 30th street and got on the #30 headed toward downtown like she normally did, but she got right off on Lake Street and walked the remainder of the way to Sid's grandmother's home.

It was super early, and she was hesitant to knock on the door even though she and Sid had already discussed this the night before. She knocked and a few moments later an older woman came to the door which was his grandmother.

"Is Sid home?" Kayla asked.

"Come on in," she said. "Sidney" she yelled calling him by his government name "You have company." She motioned for Kayla to have a seat on the couch, so she did. Immediately Kayla noticed roaches crawling around everywhere, but she still sat down and waited for Sid. She didn't even care about the roaches she just wanted to kick it with him. Sid came into the living room, he had been asleep.

"I'll be right back," he said as he went to the bathroom and turned on the water. Kayla assumed he was brushing his teeth and washing his face. He came back into the living room grinning from ear to ear. He was both happy and shocked Kayla had come. He had been trying hard to get her to come over, and she finally came.

He greeted Kayla with a "Was sup, give me a hug." Kayla got up and gave him what he wanted.

"Damn" he said admiring the way that body dress fit her body, She was small framed, but she had some nice sized breasts that showed off well in that dress. He had his hands wrapped around her waist, he got in her face and they shared their first kiss, which was everything to Kayla. He obviously wasn't ashamed of the roaches either—he acted as if they weren't even there.

They sat on the couch together and he turned to BET and they talked and watched videos and made out for hours. After a while he asked Kayla if she was hungry. She was but the shyness in her made her say no. He told her that he'd be right back. He was gone for a good hour. Kayla felt awkward sitting there in his grandmother's house while he wasn't there. The phone started ringing and Kayla just sat there.

"Answer it baby," his grandmother said from the other room. So Kayla answered it like she said.

"Is Sid there?" a female said on the other end of the phone

"No," Kayla responded. There was an awkward moment of silence.

Then the female asked, "Is this his sister?"

Kayla again said, "No." Kayla had no clue who the girl was. "Who is this?" Kayla, asked since the girl questioned her.

"Sophia," the girl answered.

Kayla had no clue who this girl Sophia was, but she was going to find out sooner than later. Finally, after about an hour of her sitting there waiting. Sid came back through the door with time-out and a bag of snacks for the two of them. They ate the food and chilled out some more. Kayla enjoyed lying on the couch with him as he held her. Kayla didn't mention the phone call that he received while he was gone, she figured that whoever it was would talk to him later, and it didn't matter to her because she was occupying his time at the moment. They kissed and Sid made a move by putting his hand up her dress and moving her panties to the side and slipping two of his fingers inside her. Then out of nowhere a lady came busting in the door singing along to the music that was playing from the TV. He quickly removed his hand.

"Hey Momma," he said to the lady.

"Hey baby," she responded as she danced and sang along to the music.

"Hey," she said this time speaking to Kayla.

Kayla spoke back, "Hey."

His mom came in and made herself comfortable joining the two kids and stayed over with them not knowing that she had cocked blocked her son. By the time she left it was time for Kayla to head back to her aunt's house. School was now over and she was already running late from the usual time she got home. She had been having so much fun that she lost track of time. She and Sid kissed again and she promised to come back over soon.

Kayla ran into Sid on her way home from school a few days later. He tried to get her to stay for a while, but she had to get home. He grabbed her, and was all up on her, kissing her and everything. She so wanted to stay, but she had been getting in trouble enough lately with her dad.

"I'll come back after I finish my homework," she promised him.

"You better come back," Sid demanded in a playful tone. He was serious though. He was trying to get in between her legs, especially since he was unsuccessful the week prior when she had skipped school to be with him the whole day. Kayla hurried home and did her homework. Once she was done, she called Sid.

"Hello," a female answered the phone. It sounded like she had been crying, her voice was shaky.

"Is Sid there?" Kayla asked with a big smile across her face. She couldn't wait to tell him that she was on her way.

"Sid, dead, Sid Gone," the female responded. Kayla was confused.

"Huh?" she said forcing the girl to repeat herself.

"He's dead, Sid gone." Kayla's heart fell to the bottom of her stomach. She couldn't believe the words she had just heard. She had just seen him an hour ago, he couldn't be dead.

Kayla jumped up and ran out of the house to head to Sid's house. She ran until her calves started to burn, then she walked as fast as she could. As soon as she hit the block she saw a crowd outside of his home.

As she walked up to the house, a little boy said, "My brother dead," all nonchalant. Kayla stood outside the entrance of the yard by the gate and cried silently to herself. Family and friends walked in and out the house all talking about what had just happened.

One man stopped and said, "You was just here the other day right?" talking to Kayla. Kayla nodded. He shook his head saying "Damn nephew, you going to be missed."

Two girls walked up, one was crying the other was comforting her. They asked what hospital he was at, and then left. For a few hours Kayla just stood there in disbelief. She really had started to take a liking to him. They hadn't spent much time together, but she was looking forward to spending more. After a while the sun started to go down, so she headed home. She didn't walk fast or run as she did on the way there. Once she hit her granny's block she stopped a few houses up at her friend's house that was with her when she first ran into Sid and told her the bad news. Then she went on home.

Ray was pissed off when she walked back through the door. She had left without asking, and he had no idea where she had gone. "Where you been," he asked.

"My friend just got killed," Kayla answered honestly.

"So what you going to do about it?" Kayla ignored him and went to her room and cried herself to sleep. The next day she didn't even want to get up to go to school, but she had no choice no one in that household had sympathy for her situation or how she felt. So off to school she went like any other morning, but she cried and cried, and cried. She was sent to her counselor's office Mrs. Crawford, it was Mrs., Crawford's first time meeting Kayla. She was very comforting, and she expressed concern for the young girl.

That day was long, but it was finally over. The next few days didn't get any better. Kayla was taking the death of

Sid very hard. She had known of him practically his whole life, but she was just getting to know him as a person. She had never experienced that type of pain before. She hadn't lost anyone close to her before. Although things between them were fairly new, it hurt her to think of what could have been. The weekend came around, and Kayla had to get up out of her granny's house. She was bored out of her mind there 24/7, Ray was barely there and she and her cousin barely got along at all. Ray wasn't okay with letting her leave that weekend for whatever reason. There was nothing in particular, just showing that he was in control not Kayla. Kayla did what she wanted anyway. Instead of going to her normal spot, Spencer Projects she went to Pleasant View to Shaun's house. That was her second go-to place to kick it at.

~

The next upcoming weekend, Ray put his foot down and kept his word when it came to his daughter. The weekend had come up again she wanted to leave, so she asked to go to her normal spots. To her surprise his answer was "No" this time. Ray telling Kayla "No" was like a foreign language to Kayla. She almost couldn't believe he said "No," so she asked again to see if he was playing and joking around with her.

It was rare that Ray told her "No" about anything, but that time he wasn't playing. However, Kayla ignored his wishes and left anyway and went to the Pleasant View projects to Shaun's house. She spent the weekend kicking it, and it was time to go home to get ready for the school week. So Kayla called her dad to come pick her up.

He shocked her when he told her "No. You wanted to be grown, now be grown and figure out what you are going to do." He hung up the phone before she could respond. Kayla had no game plan, she just knew he would come to get her once she called, but he was tired of her shit. He was the parent and if she wasn't going to listen, he wasn't going to put up with it.

Kayla stayed at Shaun's house another day, but after that she went down to her Aunt Lynn's house. She needed to go to school. Ray had calmed down some, but not all the way. He had at least sent some clothes and money down for Kayla to be able to go to school. Kayla didn't care one way or the other—she was right where she wanted to be anyway.

It took a couple of weeks for Sid's family to get his funeral arrangements together. Kayla had found out when and where the services would be held. The funeral service was going to be held at their childhood church Smith Temple. Kayla wanted to attend and her cousins Jackie, Avery, and Keisha were going to attend as moral support. Kayla had been taking his death hard. She cried constantly. They would kick it and she'd burst out crying. She hadn't been herself since he died.

Finally they thought they had gotten her mind off of Sidney for a minute, they were down at Lisa's house drinking, kicking it, playing cards, and listening to music. Kayla was downing the drinks. They had lime twisted Gin, and St. Ives Reserves. Next thing you knew Kayla was crying again. "Sidney, Sidney," she cried out over and over again. Then she threw up everywhere, and passed out on the couch. Lynn had to come get her and take her to the house.

"Who is going to clean this up?" everyone asked. "Y'all is," Lynn replied, "because y'all should have never gotten her drunk." Not one of them dared to challenge Lynn's response. They knew they were wrong. So cleaning it up was the least that they should have been worried about. If Lynn wanted to take it that far, all of their asses could have been in trouble.

When the day of Sid's funeral finally came, Kayla and her cousins attended, and that's when she found out that Sid was a player. First off, the funeral was deep, Smith Temple was packed wall to wall. That was the most people ever in that church at one time. There were several girls in attendance at his service, and they all seemed to think that they were Sid's girlfriend. Or at least they claimed to be, that was a common thing for females to do when a nigga died. They'd be quick to stake claims, but no one knew nothing of them while the person was living. Sophia was also there, she was the girl that called that day she skipped school at his house. She was big and pregnant with his unborn son. Her name was in the obituary, and she rode in the family car. Kayla still paid her respects, and placed the poem she had written for him in his casket.

Sid's twin sister wasn't taking his death well at all, she still sounded the same as she did the day he died and Kayla called on the phone. She was heartbroken; a part of her was taken away the day they killed her brother. His home boys from the neighborhood let Master P's I Miss My Homies out of their vehicles after the service. Kayla and her crew opted out of going to the grave site and repass. After the services, Kayla's personal pity party was officially over.

— 5 —

BITTERSWEET MOVE

Moving in with her aunt Lynn was bittersweet. Since she was younger she would be over at her aunt's house like clockwork every weekend. Her aunt would have knock-down drag outs with her sister Kay behind Kayla's wellbeing. Kayla and Keisha often witnessed these fights between the sisters and they would cry and hold each other for comfort. Kayla would pretend to lose her shoes, coat, or whatever in an attempt to not have to go home with Kay after the weekend ended. Sometimes Lynn would attempt to say Kayla could not spend the night, but the majority of the time, the girls begged and convinced her to allow her to stay anyway. Even if they had to offer to clean the whole house, they would do it just so Kayla could stay.

If she had had a choice she would have lived with Lynn her whole life. Keisha was Kayla's favorite cousins, but they were more like sisters. Jackie was another one of Kayla's favorite big cousins. She treated Kayla the same as she treated her own little sister. If Keisha had it, so did Kayla. So moving in with her aunt Lynn only made sense. It was always an idea for Kayla to move in and live with her favorite aunt, and cousin. Only Kayla was older now; she as a preteenager and not that little innocent girl she used to be, and things weren't quite the same. She was already having sex and had been exposed to numerous things a child her age should not have had to see or endure.

Lynn transferred Kayla's school so she could attend Benson with Keisha. That was trouble waiting to happen. It was this girl named Rosanne who had been bullying Keisha since the first day of school. The girls had it already planned to jump on the girl as soon as the transfer went through. On Kayla's first day, they confronted the girl in the courtyard at lunch time. Kayla went to swing on her, and just her luck the administrator was standing right behind her and caught her arm in midair. Her very first day at the new school, she was getting a call home. Kayla didn't care because it was in defense of her cousin and she knew she wouldn't get into any real trouble.

She and Keisha would skip classes often. Kayla would switch times to join Keisha for lunch and vice versa. They'd leave school property to walk around and do nothing. They never had money, and if they did it wasn't enough to do anything with.

Avery was also staying with Lynn at the time. She always tried to encourage the girls to go to school, do the work, and to stay on the right track.

"You can still kick it when you done," she'd say, attempting to get them to see the big picture of things. They'd do silly stuff like write letters back and forth to each other while they were in the same room. Then one day Avery decided she was moving out of town with her best friend to Georgia. Kayla and Keisha took the news hard. They did not want their big cousin to leave them. When the day came for her to leave they literally cried and pulled on her begging her to stay. They even unpacked her suitcase a few times. In the end they lost the battle and she was gone.

From that point on, things really started to change. They had gotten themselves into serious trouble in school.

The Administrator was fed up with the constant fighting, skipping, and getting sent to the office. She wanted to send Kayla to an alternative school and put Keisha on half days of school.

Kayla was no longer that young innocent child that needed protecting. She had changed over the years, and so did her relationship with her aunt. She went from being her aunt's favorite niece to her aunt's headache. It seemed like everything Kayla did agitated Lynn. Lynn had recently got back with her ex, the father of her son, and that's where her focus was. Living with her aunt had become challenging and not the fun ride she thought it would be.

Lynn had a long list of rules, and it seemed like she added to them daily. Kayla often felt like she was Cinderella, and Lynn was the evil step mother. Lynn wanted her house cleaned before bedtime, and when the girls got home from school. It didn't matter that they weren't there to make the mess; they still were responsible for cleaning. They would alternate days for cleaning the kitchen and bathroom. Lynn had this thing that if you weren't there to clean on your day, you'd have to clean the kitchen all the way back until your day again. It didn't matter what the reason was for not being there.

It was hard work to keep up with the responsibilities of keeping the house clean. Jackie and Avery were able to escape the madness of the chores by moving out of the house. Avery had moved to Georgia and Jackie had moved in with Shaun up in Pleasant View. Avery used to get so frustrated with that rule. She'd pay either Kayla or Keisha to clean the kitchen on her day when she planned on not coming home or when she just didn't want to do it. Lynn would still implement the rule and make her clean up until her day came back around. So that would be five days in a row.

Kayla tried to keep up with the chores even though she thought that they were unfair. She didn't understand why they were responsible for cleaning up after everyone, especially when they weren't even home. They'd be at school all day and had already cleaned up the night before. Then come home in the afternoon greeted by a whole new mess that they didn't make. No use complaining because there wasn't any reasoning with Lynn. What she said was what she said whether it was right or wrong. The only person who got away with stuff was Keisha. Keisha was Lynn's baby girl, and in her eyes she could do no wrong. Sometimes that worked to both of the girls' advantage. Which was cool with Kayla until it backfired, and she would end up having to pick up Keisha's slack, and do her chores and her own.

Kayla and Keisha stayed on a punishment—if it wasn't one thing it was another. From getting kicked out of school, skipping school, being somewhere they had no business being. Punishment was such a routine that the girls spent their time on punishment plotting what they were going to do when they got off. They figured they'd be right back on punishment anyway for something so they might as well have fun.

Kayla and Keisha would do random stuff. They would skip school with not a dollar in their pocket and end up walking the Benson area waiting until the end of the school day to catch their bus home. Once they did that and as soon as they got home they were busted for skipping. For whatever reason the administrator called both girls down to the office at the same time, and neither one of them were in their assigned classes. So they were busted and to make matters worse they were supposed to get off one of their many punishments that day, but their choice to skip class extended that punishment.

Then once they were supposed to be going up to Pleasant View to Shaun's house. Instead they went to a hotel with Kayla's boyfriend B.K. and his home boy. They actually had gotten away with that. Until the following weekend they were supposed to go babysit for Shaun, and Lynn said they couldn't go because Shaun and her other daughter Jackie and Renay were bad influences on the girls. So out of anger, Shaun, Jackie, and Renay made it a point to come down to Spencer and plead their case stating that they were not a bad influence. In fact, Kayla and Keisha made their own decision and they told on the girls. Lynn sent for Kayla and Keisha who were over at their friend house who stayed in the back of Spencer.

"I hate you bitches," Keisha screamed at the top of her lungs. Then she went outside refusing to accept the brand new punishment they had received. Kayla on the other hand didn't say anything; she just went upstairs and accepted that they were on yet another punishment. It was always something that kept them on a lockdown. However, sometimes they didn't have to do nothing at all. Lynn made them prisoners once because she and her boyfriend Roby had a falling out, and she put him out. So Kayla and Keisha couldn't go outside because she didn't want him to pull up and see them outside. That lasted for over a week and she finally allowed them to leave and go to Shaun's with Jackie and Renee.

The girls were trying to grow up too fast. The party life had become fun and addicting, and that's all that really mattered to them. Their Aunt Marie tried to interfere and get them to see things differently. One day she came down to the house.

"Let's go get a drink," she told the girls. They looked at her as if she was crazy, but they went along with it. Marie took them to Dailey's and let them pick out whatever they wanted to drink. Kayla got a bottle of Asti, and Keisha got a bottle of Alize. Marie even brought them some Black & Milds.

"Yeah, we about to get messed up," Marie kept saying, pumping the girls up. They initially thought that she was joking, but after she actually brought the stuff for them they were convinced. Once they made it back to the house she had them pour a glass of their drinks. The moment they raised those cups of liquor to their mouths. She stopped them, it was all trick like they originally thought. They should have known better than to think for one second Marie was going to condone that behavior. Marie and Lynn enjoyed the alcoholic beverages, and as far as the Black & Milds, Marie told them just hold them up to their mouth and pretend to smoke them if they wanted to look cool. The girls laughed at their aunt as she fake smoked the cigar in the plastic, saying "I'm cool. Yeah, I'm cool."

Marie had good intentions, but her plan didn't work. It was too late. They had already been accustomed to the life of kicking it and there was no stopping them.

～

A while later they met a girl named Gina who had recently moved to the projects with her mom and younger brother and sister. Keisha had a thing for her brother Shaun and those two quickly became a thing. Gina was pretty cool and the two girls looked up to her. She was very impressive to them. She was a few years older and had a little more experience than they did. She told them all sorts of stories about her and dudes she messed around with.

When they weren't up at Shaun's or over Lisa's they were in the back hanging with Gina. She did their hair and they shared clothes, and hung out on a regular. The girls would often skip school and hang out with her all day. Jackie and Shaun didn't care for Gina. However Jackie ended up being right about Gina.

First Gina started loaning out clothes she borrowed from Kayla and Keisha. Then she set Kayla up by inviting her over while Stacy's girlfriend was there. She knew Kayla had messed around with Stacy and she also knew his girlfriend Kenyatta from 29th street. So she called Kayla and Keisha over there and brought up Stacy to get Kayla to talk about him and next thing Kayla knew is that she was into an argument with this random girl that she didn't know. However, when Kayla showed no fear and stood up for herself, the girl backed down and she and Kayla actually became cool.

First Kayla and Gina fell out, and Keisha was still friends with her. Gina still hadn't replaced Kayla's shirt and pants that she borrowed, so Kayla took it upon herself to rip up a shirt that she let Keisha wear and threw it out the project window. Gina was pissed and came to Lynn's house to try to fight Kayla, that's when Lynn intervened and after that Keisha had to choose sides. Just like that their temporary friendship had ended. Gina wasn't a friend anyway because come to find out she started fucking Stacey after she stirred up all the drama with her so called friend Kenyatta and Kayla.

Shaun's unit in Pleasant View was just like Lisa's in Spencer. It was always a party with an open door policy. All the hood niggas had a place to come hang out, chill, smoke, drink, and even sleep if they needed to. From day one it had been a house party. Kayla and Keisha were always the designated babysitters.

One day they were at the house by themselves, and a dude from the hood named Chatman came by. He sparked a blunt with the girls, then he propositioned them. "I'll take y'all to the mall to go shopping, if one of y'all just let me stick it in".

"Hell naw," they both responded in unison. Then Kayla said "Take us shopping first" just to see if he was serious. Just like she thought, he wasn't, " you gotta let me fuck first". He thought just because the girls were young they would fall for his game. He was cool to kick it with and get high with, but that was about it. Neither one of the girls we even a slight bit interested in him, no matter how much money he threw in their faces. He wasn't the type to just give up easily though, he kept on trying, but his attempts failed each time.

Then he went as far as to get Kayla while she was sleeping. Kayla had slept in the room with her cousin Renay and her kids one night. Just like the incident at Lisa's house with Eric she woke up to someone licking in her ear. That time she hopped up and flicked on the light.

"What are you doing in here? You nasty muthafucka" she said, waking up her cousin Renay and the kids. Chatman sat there with a dumb look on his face. He got put on the crib that night, but he continued to come over. No one wanted to fuck with him, but he finally was able to slide his way in Shaun's panties.

— *6* —

LITTLE SISTERS

Shaun and Lisa had become like big sisters to Kayla and Keisha. Not only did they babysit their kids, but they built a bond. However, that bond was tested by a nigga. Shaun had started messing around with JD, unaware that Kayla once had something going on with JD that never quite ended. Nevertheless, they started messing around.

JD was only sixteen years old, and Shaun was 25 and really had no business messing with him anyway. The age difference didn't matter because he was the new boo. Kayla never spoke about the relationship she had with JD, and she just sat back and watched her big-sister figure and her ex sex partner be together. JD would come over to Shaun's house while she was out at the club, eat her food, and talk about her like a dog. He'd talk about her house being dirty, the way she kept her kids, and more. Kayla and Keisha would just laugh at him, because he wasn't lying. JD was just using her for what she had to offer, which was some of her ADC check and her food stamps.

Of course he was in it for the sex. He was just 16 and fucking a 25-year-old woman. His ego was definitely being stroked. Shaun would act a fool behind JD. When she would come home from the bar and he wasn't at her place waiting for her, she'd go looking for him.

"Oh he ain't here, let's go" she would say to Kayla or Keisha who would tag along as she searched for this nigga on foot. The two girls were young and didn't mind following behind their makeshift big sister for the show they knew was in store once she found him.

JD and Shaun's relationship didn't last too long. For one, he couldn't deal with her aggressiveness, and her obsessive behavior. She acted like she was his momma rather than his girlfriend. Second, he and Kayla still had a thing going on secretly. When Shaun fell asleep, JD snuck out of her room many nights to lie up, and mess with Kayla. One day, JD and Kayla hooked up at her Aunt Lynn's house while she was gone. Kayla told Keisha about the hook up, who betrayed her and told Jackie.

One day as the group was hanging in Spencer sitting on the stoop, Jackie jumped up out of nowhere and said "Shaun, Kayla has something to tell you."

Shaun stared at Kayla, waiting for her to say something. Kayla was confused. Then Jackie blurted, "Kayla and JD slept together."

Kayla was speechless. Shaun was outraged, "What? You was like my sister; how could you?" Jackie happily filled in all the details that Keisha had shared with her. Shaun told Kayla that she didn't want to have nothing else to do with her and that she wasn't welcome in her house anymore either. Shaun was mad, but Renee quickly shut her down a bit when she let Shaun know that in fact Kayla and JD had messed around long before she came about.

Unknown to any of them—even JD—was that Kayla was once pregnant by him and that she had miscarried the baby. This was information that Kayla kept to herself.

Shaun set her mind to hurt Kayla the way she had been hurt, so she decided to go to Lynn and disclose some other information. She pretended to be concerned about Kayla, but if that was true, she would have taken some action when she first heard about it. A while back, the girls were at Shaun's house paying a game called crazy hearts. The rules were that if you got a heart you had to answer a question truthfully, and if someone else in the room knew the truth they were allowed to disclose the truth if the player with the heart card didn't. They had played crazy hearts many times before, but that particular time a well-kept secret came out about Kayla's older cousin molesting her courtesy of Keisha who thought it was funny. Shaun was disgusted with the revelation and immediately stopped playing the game, but she never mentioned it again. It was only when she found out about Kayla and JD that she decided to say something to Lynn.

— 7 —

SWEEPING IT UNDER THE RUG AGAIN

Kayla was both embarrassed and relieved at the same time when the secret came out. Her cousin Ricky had been molesting her for so long it had become normal. It was like a routine part of her life that she just dealt with on her own. She was now old enough to know that it was wrong, but she didn't know how to stop it. She was afraid to speak up and tell anyone, because she had always felt like it was her fault that it had been happening. She felt like she had allowed it and that she would be the one in trouble if she spoke up about it.

So Shaun had actually helped her out, even though her intentions were to hurt her.

After the secret had been revealed, Kayla was confronted by her aunt Lynn, her aunt Marie and her grandmother June via telephone. At first Kayla hesitated to speak on the subject out of embarrassment, so she said that it wasn't true. Aunt Marie asked, "Well how come when we asked Ricky he started crying and apologizing?"

Finally Kayla broke down and told the truth. She went back to the very first time when she was just a little girl. She recounted every single event as tears streamed down her face. Her aunts and grandmother were silent on the phone listening to her tell her story. When she was done no one knew the words to say to comfort her.

Finally, after years of the abuse she didn't have to hold that secret inside anymore. After she poured her heart out to them, her worst fears came true, and the accusations began.

"It's your fault, you knew better."

"Why didn't you tell someone?"

Many more questions followed that day, however, after that conversation nothing else was spoken about it. It was like it never happened. Just like every other abused person in the family, her story was swept under the rug as well.

Kayla regretted her decision to tell the truth, because it didn't make her situation any better. She began to feel worse than she had when she was holding the information inside. It was ironic, because out of all the things Kayla endured and was exposed to with her mother, Kay, not one time was Kayla touched in an inappropriate or sexual way while in her care. This happened within her own blood family with people that she loved and trusted the most.

For a moment during the phone conversation with her aunts and grandmother, Kayla saw a flicker of hope that she would finally be able to open up about the abuse she endured over the years. Ricky hadn't been the first in the family to violate her. There were two older cousins, but Kayla had managed to escape them during their attempt, after which they left her alone. Kayla wished she could share all of those secrets that she held inside, but she could not. It wasn't that her family didn't believe her, they just didn't know how to handle the situation. The adults were aware of it, they'd have to do something, and they would rather not have to do anything about it. Kayla secretly hated her family for their response to her abuse, but she went with the flow because her family was all she had, and all she knew.

Some girls have no choice, but to grow up fast. It started with June, then Kay and her siblings, now it was happening to Kayla. Most likely it had carried on from generation to generation before June. From being introduced to sex at a young age, to caring for themselves when in fact someone should have been caring for them. Innocence gone too soon, and it was a cycle that kept repeating itself in this family.

After the secret was known by her family, it seemed like living with Lynn got even more difficult for Kayla. Lynn was on her for everything she did. Kayla felt like she couldn't do anything right by her Aunt. She'd come home from school, and randomly Lynn would say, "You can't go outside today."

When Kayla questioned why, the excuses were that she didn't wash the walls or clean the refrigerator. It became frustrating for Kayla, who began to rebel because she felt her Aunt was not being fair. One day after being told she could not go outside, Lynn caught Kayla outside hitting a cigarette, and made her come inside. Kayla had had it. She decided that she wasn't going to be on a punishment behind that. Especially considering the day before her aunt allowed her to smoke and said nothing.

~

Kayla continued to endure more pain and hurt from someone trying to violate her and nothing happening about it. One afternoon, Kayla was chilling at Lisa's house like she had started doing. She fell asleep sitting on her couch. Suddenly, she felt someone licking in her ear. She jumped up startled to realize it was Eric, an old cat that Lisa had been messing around with. He was from down south and he swore up and down that before he came to Nebraska he used to hang out with Master P. No one ever believed him, but he never backed down off his story.

"What are you doing? Get off of me," Kayla screamed "Lisa, Lisa!" she yelled until Lisa came out of the kitchen.

"What's wrong Kayla, what's going on?" she asked confused.

"Get your man, he was in here licking in my ear while I was asleep," she told Lisa. Eric had jumped back over to the other couch trying to pretend that he was asleep and that he didn't know what was going on.

"He ain't asleep" Kayla yelled.

"Eric, what's going on?" Lisa asked as she pushed on him, waking him up out of his fake sleep.

He played dumb. "I don't know what she talking about." Kayla was hysterical and angry she wasn't about to play his games. Kayla looked at her friend—someone who claimed to be like a big sister to her—and told her again what had happened.

Lisa's response was just, "Well Kayla maybe he didn't mean anything by it".

Kayla looked at her with disgust. She was at a loss for words for a moment. Her anger then went from Eric to Lisa. She cursed her ass out. "Are you that desperate for a man?" she questioned. "Bitch you ain't shit, I'm sitting here telling you that this man touched me inappropriately and you have the nerves to be trying to make excuses and take up for him?"

Kayla's feelings were hurt. She could not believe what had just happened. She never thought that she would get that kind of reaction from someone she thought she was close to. That little sister shit seemed to go out of the window quickly when it came to some dick. Shaun and Lisa showed

Kayla where their loyalties were. Kayla vowed to herself to never be that type of bitch. So desperate for a nigga that she allowed fuck shit to go on.

Lisa didn't want to believe it. She was in love with Eric and she couldn't see past that.

Kayla didn't talk to Lisa for a long time after that. It wasn't until Eric started sleeping with a couple of her other "so called" friends and ended up getting one pregnant when she realized that Eric truly wasn't shit. She apologized to Kayla for not believing her and being there for her as a big sister figure should have.

COMPETITION & PAYBACK

Thanksgiving 1998 was a celebration like always. Lynn cooked up a feast with enough food to feed the entire Spencer projects. Lynn was feeling good, and she in was in such a good mood that she did something that she had never done. She opened her house to a few of the young project niggas to come in and join the party.

On a regular day they weren't allowed to sit on her porch or even stand in front of her unit. Lynn didn't play that, she knew they were all hustlers or banned and barred from OHA property, and she wasn't risking getting evicted for none of them. It was Fats, JD, Slim, Rico, and Michael; and by nightfall, it became a house party in Lynn's living room.

Kayla and Keisha got a pass that night and was able to smoke their little black & milds and sip on a little drank. Any other time they had to sneak to do those things, but that night they didn't. The music was playing all of their favorite cuts from Public Announcement (Yippie-Yi-Yo), Montell Jordan (Let's ride) to Deborah Cox's (Nobody supposed to be here), and Playa (Cheers to you). The unit was bumping, and everyone was having a good time.

Anne came over, and she was ready to party. She came right through the door dancing and swinging her big ol' butt. She immediately picked Michael out of the group and it was on from that point. She started to seduce him with her dance moves and grinding. At first, he seemed hesitant, but Anne was showing him what she was working with, and he quickly gained interest. Kayla took notice to the interaction her aunt and Michael were having, but she ignored it. In her mind her aunt was too old for him, and they were just dancing. What harm could that cause? She thought to herself. Unbeknownst to Kayla, it wasn't just innocent dancing, and the two had made plans to leave together that night.

Once the partying wound down, everyone went back to their normal activities. Kayla went outside, and she spotted her aunt Anne's car at the corner exiting the projects. She saw someone on the passenger side, but she assumed it was Anne's daughter. The next morning Kayla realized that it may have been Michael in the car, because she learned that Anne's daughter had spent the night at her cousin Tracy's house. Kayla thought back to the silhouette of the passenger in her Aunt's car. The events of the night before flashed in her mind, and she remembered all the flirtatious dancing Anne and Michael were doing. Her heart silently broke at the thoughts that she was having. There was no doubt in her mind that her Aunt and Michael had slept together. She planned to find out if her suspicions were true.

She confronted Michael as he sat in the car with the home boy Fats smoking a blunt. "So, did you fuck my aunt?" she bluntly asked with a straight face.

Michael couldn't keep himself from smirking as he lied and said no.

So Kayla asked him again, "It isn't funny. Did you fuck my aunt?"

He rolled up the window and she could see his mouth moving, and Fats laughing. It was obvious that he said yeah once he rolled the window up, because Fats wasn't laughing for no reason. He rolled it back down and looked at Kayla and bold-face lied again. At that moment Kayla knew she was going to get revenge.

It just so happened that on that same day she would get her chance.

After confronting Michael, Kayla was certain that he and her aunt had had sex. He didn't have to say the words—his actions told it all. He thought the situation was funny, but Kayla didn't find anything funny. Her feelings were hurt, and she was mad at the both of them. Michael knew how she felt about him, and he played on her feelings constantly. Anne hadn't a clue that she stepped on her niece's toes, but she was going to soon find out. The next time she showed her face Kayla didn't have two words to say to her. Her ignore game was strong towards Anne. Anne couldn't figure out what she had done wrong. The last time they had any issues was when she put her niece out, but that was a thing of the past. Since then they had reconciled and hung out together a few times. Anne was one of the cooler aunts—when Kayla wasn't living with her. Anne liked to hang out and kick it just like her nieces did. She actually had more in common with her nieces than with her sisters. Her nieces helped her feel young again. She had to ask around to find out what Kayla's issue with her was. Eventually she found out from Jackie that it was about Michael.

"Kayla, I know you are mad at me. Whatever you think happened with me and Michael did, but I want you to know that I didn't know anything about you two. I love you and I am truly sorry. I hope that you can forgive me. I know it won't change what happened, but I will leave him alone if that means you will forgive me." Anne cried real tears as she gave her niece the sincere heartfelt apology. Kayla just gave her a blank stare as tears streamed down her face. Deep down she believed Anne, but she wasn't quite ready to forgive her aunt.

In Kayla's mind she felt that her aunt should have been ashamed of herself. She was damn near old enough to be his mother. Anne's own son was only 2-3 years younger than him. In reality he was too young for Anne, but too old for Kayla. However, they had already crossed that line so age was no longer an factor. That was just what she was known for, the type of antics she pulled that night. True enough, Michael played a huge role in it as well, he knew he and Kayla had a thing—Anne did not. Kayla still chose to focus her anger on her Aunt. In Kayla's mind Michael belonged to her, was her man.

At the end of the day Kayla's lust for Michael made her place full blame on Anne. She felt that her Aunt threw herself on him, and it was only natural for him to take the bait. It was like putting a steak in front of a lion, you better believe that lion was going to eat; and that's exactly what happened.

Jackson was a young hustler from the projects. He, his mom, and sister lived in the back of Spencer. Kayla always noticed him around the projects and thought that he was cute. He was all the girls used to talk about "Jackson this, Jackson that" Kayla was a few years younger than him, so besides seeing him around the projects she didn't really know him. He was a caramel colored nigga, brush cut, small framed, with eyes to die for. Then Kayla met his cousin Michael, and she only had eyes for him. That is, until he slept with her aunt Anne. She was beyond hurt about that situation, and her young mind could only think of how she could get back at him.. Michael thought that she was young and dumb. Yes, she was young, but she was not dumb—naïve and immature even, but definitely not dumb.

Kayla and Keisha were a few door down at the home girl Lisa's house babysitting as they did on a regular. Once the kids fell asleep it was their time to kick it. Jackson and Fats stopped by to smoke a blunt with the girls. Jackson had a bottle of Asti that he shared with them also. After smoking a Garcia Vega green leaf blunt, and drinking the bottle of Asti, they all fucked off for a few, talking and listening to music.

Jackson and Kayla sat on the stairs talking, and playing around with each other. Only thing that was in their way at that moment was Keisha who was unknowingly cock blocking.

"Go change the radio," Kayla suggested, which distracted her cousin as she went to change the radio station. That was their moment to escape her presence. In the short time it took her to turn the radio station, Kayla and Jackson had snuck off to one of the upstairs bedrooms where they started tongue kissing each other. Before you knew it they were both butt naked having sex. It was crazy because they both had a physical attraction to one another He had been checking for her, but his cousin had already pushed up on her. So he sat back in the cut, and let the situation work itself out. However, on this night, he and Kayla were both tipsy and she was sending all kind of vibes his way. Touching him seductively, grabbing his dick, and everything.

Jackson probably knew that she was only giving him this extra attention because of Michael and her aunt, and he was taking advantage of that. Although Kayla did kind of like him, he was fine. Whether this opportunity was a rebound or payback, he didn't much care at the moment. His dick was rock hard and he was with it. Only once they started having sex though, a few minutes into it, he started to feel guilty—or at least he pretended to feel guilty.

Right in the middle, he said, "This don't feel right, you MoMo's girl." Then he just stopped in the middle and got up, he got dressed quickly and said, "I'm sorry;" and left Kayla naked, confused, and disappointed at the same time. She couldn't understand where that came from.

"Fuck Michael," she said to herself, she didn't belong to him. He made his choice when he slept with her aunt. Now she was sleeping with his cousin, what was there to feel guilty about? Once Kayla got her thoughts together and got her clothes back on. She joined her cousin back downstairs, and tried to act like nothing happened.

"What were y'all doing?" Keisha asked Kayla as if she didn't already know. Kayla gave her favorite cousin the run down on everything that happened, except for the end. She told Keisha that he nutted fast, rather than telling her that he had a sudden guilt trip and stopped in the middle. Low-key after thinking about it she kind of figured that's what actually happened and he was ashamed to admit it, so he played it off like he felt guilty. It was what it was.

The next day came, and when Kayla saw Jackson, he acted normal and nonchalant about what had happened the night before. It was like it never happened. He smoked with her and her cousins like always and chopped it up. When Michael showed his face, Kayla showed him absolutely no love. He came up with grinning "wad up?"

Everyone replied except for Kayla, who rolled her eyes something viscous. Her look said it all and that was a big "FUCK YOU!"

Michael smirked and said, "Like that," looking and directing his comment at Kayla. She straight-up ignored him and took a puff of her black and mild. He laughed it off and walked off down the street.

From that day forward Kayla was over Michael; he had truly hurt her heart. It was one thing that he fucked with other females, but her aunt! She wasn't with that at all.

As a car rolled by one day, Kayla moved to the music that was coming from its windows. Out of nowhere Lynn said, "Don't be shaking your ass in front of my man." Kayla couldn't believe what Lynn had just said that to her—she was barely moving, dancing wasn't even her thing. She was definitely shy when it came to dancing in front of people. That statement caught her completely off guard, and Kayla was definitely not thinking about Lynn's man. Keisha danced all the time and she wouldn't have dared to say something like that to her. And besides, even if she was dancing, Lynn's man had no business looking at Kayla in that way anyway.

That was another sign that showed Lynn's feelings changing towards her niece. Kayla didn't know how to deal with her aunt's change of attitude with her. It was like she was constantly walking on eggshells. On her way out one afternoon, Lynn asked Kayla to grab her purse out of her room. "But make sure you knock first," Lynn told Kayla.

Kayla did as requested, she knocked on the bedroom door and announced herself.

"Come on in," Rick said. So she opened the door and went inside. She walked around the bed to the side table to grab her aunt's purse. Rick had his finger to his mouth signaling her to hush and pointed to the TV screen which was playing a porno. Instead of turning it off or turning the channel when he told Kayla to come in, he just paused the TV. Unfortunately, it just so happened to be on a scene when the woman had the man's penis in her mouth. Kayla turned her face up in disgust. Then she grabbed Lynn's purse and exited the room. She decided it would be wise to not mention what had just happened. In Kayla's experience, she feared that somehow the tables would be turned and she would be blamed for his inappropriate behavior.

After that incident Rick would always smile at Kayla and try to get her to give him a hug, but he was just too friendly in Kayla's eyes, and that had always been dangerous for her. Her aunt would have most likely found some way to blame Kayla for hitting on her man…

She ignored him and laughed off his request each and every time. He was smart about it though; he never made such a request in Lynn's presence. He knew she would have fucked his ass up if she caught him acting a fool. However, Kayla believed he was part of the reason her aunt's feelings changed about her. She may have not spoken on it, but she knew her man, and she knew him well.

— 9 —

FEELING LIKE CINDERELLA

Growing up, Kayla had been her Aunt Lynn's favorite niece. She'd have some knock down, drag outs with Kay behind her niece. If Kayla had a choice in the matter she would have moved in with Lynn and grew up with her favorite cousin Keisha. Now that Kayla was growing up and a teenager, Lynn wasn't as protective of her as she once was. She took her in her house, but that came with a high price to pay.

Ever since Ricky was exposed, it seemed that everything Kayla did agitated Lynn. Kayla had made it almost a whole year staying with her aunt, but that year was challenging. Lynn had a long list of rules, and it seemed like she added to them daily. Kayla started to feel like she was Cinderella. Lynn demanded that her house be cleaned when the girls got home from school and before bedtime. It didn't matter that they weren't there to make the mess; they still were responsible for cleaning up. The girls alternated days for cleaning the kitchen and bathroom. Lynn had this thing that if you weren't there to clean on your day, you'd have to clean the kitchen all the way back until your day again. It didn't matter what the reason was for not being there.

It was really hard work being responsible for cleaning in Lynn's house, due to all the extra added on rules she made up. Avery and Jackie had escaped the madness. Avery moved to Georgia and Jackie moved in with Shaun up in Pleasant view. Avery used to get so frustrated with that "missed day" rule. She'd pay either Kayla or Keisha to clean the kitchen on her day when she planned on not coming home or when she just didn't want to do it. Lynn would still implement the rule and make her clean up until her day came back around. That meant five days in a row, and that was not fun.

Kayla tried to keep up with the chores even though she thought that they were unfair. She didn't understand why she and Keisha were responsible for cleaning up after everyone, especially when they weren't even home. Clean up at night, go to bed, get up and go to school all day, and then come home to be greeted by a whole new mess that they didn't make. There was no use complaining because there was no reasoning with Lynn. What she said was law, rather it was right or wrong. She had no problems letting people know just that. No matter how hypocritical it was.

The only person who got away with stuff was Keisha. Keisha was Lynn's baby girl and in her eyes she could do no wrong. Sometime that worked to both girls' advantage. Which was cool with Kayla until it backfired, and Kayla ended up having to pick up Keisha's slack and do her chores in addition to her own.

The two cousins stayed continuously on a punishment. If it wasn't one thing it was another—from getting kicked out of school, skipping school, being somewhere they had no business being. Punishment was such a part of their routine that the girls spent the time on punishment plotting what they were going to do when they got off. They figured they'd be right back on punishment anyway for something so they might as well have fun.

Kayla and Keisha got in trouble for random stuff. They would skip school with not a dollar in their pocket and end up walking the Benson area waiting until the end of the school day to catch their bus home. One such adventure they were busted for skipping as soon as they got home that afternoon. For whatever reason during the school day, the administrator had called both girls down to the office at the same time, and neither one of them were in their assigned classes. So they were busted, and to make matters worse, they were set to get off one of their many punishments that day.

Another time, they were supposed to be going up to Pleasant View to Shaun's house. Instead they went to a hotel with Kayla's boyfriend B.K. and his home boy. B.K. was a senior in high school and she was a freshman. Kayla met him when they started hanging out in Pleasant View projects. B.K. was a light skinned pretty boy. B.K.'s real name was Brian, they named him B.K. short for Blood Killer since he was a crip. He was a hustler just like most of the dudes who hung out in the projects. He was one of the niggas who didn't have to be in the streets, but he chose to. He came from a solid family who cared about him, but he still succumbed to the street life. He drove a freshly-painted gold box Chevy that was on some rims with the beats. Kayla thought she was the shit messing around with him. There she was, a freshman with a senior boyfriend and he had his own car.

However, Jackie didn't like him and she took every opportunity to let him know that she didn't like him. They were always arguing when he came around. Kayla would just sit there and say nothing. She knew there was no winning when it came to her cousin Jackie, so she didn't even try.

The girls had actually had gotten away with going to the hotel that day. Jackie wasn't happy about it and she talked her usual shit, but that was it. The following weekend, they were supposed to go babysit for Shaun, but Lynn said they couldn't go because Shaun, Jackie, and Renay were bad influences on the girls. So out of anger Shaun, Jackie, and Renay walked down to Spencer and pleaded their case that they were not bad influences, and in fact Kayla and Keisha made their own decision to go to the hotel.

Lynn sent for Kayla and Keisha who were at their friend Gina's house in the back of Spencer.

"I hate you bitches," Keisha screamed at the top of her lungs to the three older girls. Then she went outside refusing to accept the brand new punishment they had received. Kayla on the other hand didn't say anything; she just went upstairs and accepted that they were on yet another punishment. There was always something that kept them on a lock down. However, sometimes they did nothing at all to earn the punishment. Lynn made them prisoners once because she and her man Ricky had a falling out, and she put him out. So Kayla and Keisha couldn't go outside because she didn't want him to pull up and see them outside. That lasted for over a week and she finally allowed them to leave and go to Shaun's with Jackie and Renay.

~

Lynn had put her niece out once again. It seemed as if this time she was serious. Kayla however, was not trying to go live in a group home or with somebody she didn't know. She had burned her bridges with most of the family members, and those she hadn't burned her bridges with just didn't have the time to take her in. Everyone was busy with their own lives and their own children. So Kayla was on the run.

Shaun put her anger about the past with JD aside and allowed Kayla to stay at her project unit in Pleasant view.

She felt sorry for Kayla, and over the months she had rebuilt a bond with her and her family. No matter how angry she had been about JD, Kayla was in need and Shaun couldn't leave her hanging. Kayla was more than her babysitter—she was like a little sister and her little home girl, regardless of what transpired. She was the adult in the situation. It helped that she and JD were no longer dealing with each other. It took her no time to realize that he was just using her, and lying to her—just like many of the men she'd come across…

Kayla stayed hidden at Shaun's apartment for about a week before Lynn grew suspicious. She had been inquiring about her niece's whereabouts since Kayla had ran off. She knew that if Kayla wasn't at any of the family houses that she had to be somewhere close. Everyone pretended not to know, in an attempt to protect Kayla, and buy some time while Lynn cooled off, and changed her mind and take her niece back in.

The plan was going smoothly until Shaun's daughter Aliyah spilled the beans. Kayla liked Shaun's only daughter; she was one of her favorite out of all the kids. She bought Aliyah stuff, comb her hair, she treated that little girl like she was her own child. That's exactly how Lynn figured out where her niece was staying. Lynn went a few doors down to Lisa's house and she noticed Aliyah had a new hair style. She knew Shaun hadn't done it. So she asked the little girl, "Who did your hair?"

Aliyah answered, "Kayla." Being only 2 years old she didn't understand that she was telling on Kayla.

"Uh huh, busted! I knew y'all was hiding her!" Lynn said to Shaun. Lynn then threatened that if they continued to hide her that she would call the police. And considering she was a minor and a ward of the state, Shaun felt bad for Kayla, but she couldn't be involved in that situation.

Kayla cried when Shaun and her cousin Jackie broke the news to her. She understood their position, but she had nowhere to go. She felt hopeless and she just cried and cried. The next day she made her way back down to Spencer to turn herself in. Kayla went to Lisa's house and sent Jackie and Shaun to notify Lynn where she was.

Lisa's sister, Kim, was visiting her sister and her niece and nephews at the house just then. She inquired about what was going on, and her heart broke when she heard the situation that Kayla was in. Just like that, no second thoughts or anything, Kim agreed to take Kayla in.

Kim was 29 years old and had two children. She owned and operated her own in home daycare, and she knew she'd have no problem getting temporary custody of Kayla. Lynn was not happy at all about that situation. She tried to discourage Kim from taking her in, but her attempts were unsuccessful.

"Umm, you don't know what you're getting yourself into," Lynn said. "She's a handful, got an attitude, and fast as she want to be." Lynn went on an on down talking her niece right in her face. All that did was make Kim want to take her in more. Kim couldn't believe the negative things Lynn said about her own niece. Kayla was hurt by her aunt's words, but she refused to break in her presence and give her any satisfaction. Kayla just stood there silently—but if looks could kill, Lynn would have died instantly.

Kayla's eyes where scrunched up, her face was tense; she stood with her fist balled up. It took everything in Kayla to stay silent and listen to how her aunt felt about her. Lynn left with an attitude and said, "Good luck!"

As soon as she left, Kayla broke down into tears. The things her aunt said to her and about her were heartbreaking. Before that scene she had hoped her aunt would change her mind and let her come back to live, but after that she didn't want to go back.

The moment Kayla moved into Kim's house, Kim was eager and determined to be a positive person in her life. Her personal goal was to change the young girl's life around. Kim took her in and tried to get her back on the right track. After her Aunt Lynn gave up on her and put her out.

Kim wanted show Kayla that she was loved, and that even though life had been unfair to her for quite some time it was going to get better. From the first time Kim had met Kayla she could see the pain and hurt in her eyes. Kayla was her new project, and she welcomed her into her home with open arms. It was like Kayla gained a new family immediately. Kim's sister, Lisa, was already like family to Kayla. Over the months of babysitting and hanging out at her house they had grown a bond and became close. Kayla was like a little sister to Lisa.

Living with Kim, Kayla gained two siblings. Kayla was grateful that Kim had taken her into her home. It was a breath of fresh air. Staying with her aunt had become hard and stressful. Ever since she got back with her ex, she had been treating Kayla like the evil step child rather than her favorite niece. Growing up, Kayla had been a only child, so she didn't really know how it felt to have siblings. Tae and Keyah took a liking to Kayla as well. They were excited to have a big sister around.

Kim wasted no time at all getting the ball rolling with Kayla. She made sure she signed Kayla up for summer school so that she could pick up a few credits that she didn't get during the school year. Freshman year had been a flop for Kayla. She had completed the year with one whole credit to show for it. After her transfer from Central to Benson, she basically skipped every class the remainder of the year, if she didn't skip she just didn't do any of the work. Kim also got her signed up for the summer Job program for youth, so that she could earn some money for herself, and to help keep her busy during the summer. Everything started off smoothly without any issues.

Kayla didn't waste any time giving Kim a run for her money. Kim got way more than she bargained for. It wasn't that Kayla was bad, she had just grown used to doing her own thing for so long that getting used to rules and expectations was hard. Kim's kids were still small so she wasn't quite ready to handle a teenager. Her first misstep was way before Kayla moved in. Kim had sat at her sister's house and got drunk with Kayla one night. She knew she was underage but she thought she was older than 13 at the time. Although Kim meant no harm, she didn't know that Kayla would eventually be her responsibility. That night set the tone for their relationship. Kayla thought it would be cool to do the same things she was doing prior to moving in with Kim.

When Kayla moved in, Kim tried to switch up and stop Kayla from doing things she was already doing, such as smoking weed, cigarettes, black & mild's, and drinking. Even though Kayla was away from her stomping grounds she found a way to participate in the activities that she was used to.

Kayla would go down the street to Toot's house and smoke her cigarettes and get high. Toot was a local rap artist in a group called Drama Life. He was a cool dude and Kayla had a secret little crush on him. So she made her way down the block every chance she got just to hang out and do her thing. There were often a lot of dudes hanging out rapping in the home made studio. It was like a free concert every time she went over there. Toot was dating Kim's best friend at the time, so she too had a casual relationship with him. So when she discovered that Kayla was going down there to smoke and kick it, she made it a point to call Toot personally and request that he not smoke or drink with Kayla because she was underage. Kim had good intentions, but that didn't stop anything. Kayla would still go down there and smoke and drink and hang out. Toot would even go to the store and buy cigarettes for her from time to time.

A few months went by before Kayla was able to start hanging out in Spencer again. At first Kim was reluctant to let her go. Kim knew that she would most likely be doing stuff she shouldn't be doing. However, she ended up giving in to Kayla's request, because Kayla wasn't letting it go. She was constantly asking for permission to go down there.

It was a typical day in the projects, hanging out on the stoop smoking weed, and black and mild's with all the hood niggas. Jackson was one of the niggas out that day, and Kayla started flirting a little bit with him just for fun.

"You going to give me some dick," she said boldly and all nonchalant. Like that was just an everyday statement.

~

He gave her a quick "yeah," caught off guard by her request. Nevertheless he was with it. Fat's nosey ass was in the mix shocked by the statement she had made. He knew nothing about Kayla and Jackson messing around so he was surprised. He was also surprised because he knew first hand that Kayla was in love with Michael. The girl had dissed him for Michael even after he hated on his homie telling her how Michael didn't have good intentions with her from the jump.

He smirked, "Umm hmm," he hummed. He just looked with that silly-ass smirk plastered on his face. Even if he was to say something Kayla didn't care she didn't owe anybody any explanations. Low-key she was hoping that he did say something to Michael--then Michael would might know how she felt. That wasn't likely to be the case though; he was used to sharing bitches with his homies. One of their favorite slogans was, "Ain't no fun if the homies can't have none."

Jackson wasn't just one of the homies, though; that was family so it may have been a difference. Kayla was sure that Fats was going to let the cat out of the bag and speak on the incident. Either way Kayla had no care in the world whether he did or didn't, and apparently neither did Jackson because his response didn't show that he did.

Since their first encounter at Lisa's house, Jackson and Kayla hadn't spoken about their situation. It was their little secret. Outside of those two, Keisha was the only other person to know about their hookup. She wasn't going to say nothing unless they ended up playing another game of crazy hearts. Then it wasn't a promise that she'd keep the secret. Jackson didn't want his cousin to know that he had stepped on his toes and Kayla just didn't want everybody all up in her business. She could not care less about what Michael thought. He didn't take her feelings into consideration when he slept with her aunt.

As far as aunt Anne she had finally forgiven her after months of being angry. When Anne first apologized Kayla wasn't moved not one bit. However it wasn't like Anne intentionally stepped on her toes. She hadn't a clue prior to hooking up with Michael that her own niece had something going on with Michael. Kayla got her payback with Jackson and she moved on. At least that's what she told herself, but Michael had her in a trance. At least she felt like she had gotten payback. In reality she was just building a reputation for herself. Being young she didn't see it that way. Society had an different expectation for girls than boys. So what was seen as cool or cute for the boys, the same thing would cause the girls to be referred to as hood rats and hoes. No matter how hard she tried to be angry with him she just couldn't fully get him out of her system. She tried to play hard to get, and keep herself distracted from him by fucking around with his cousin.

After a day of kicking it in the projects, Kayla had to get back home to Kim's house. The sun had gone down and it was getting late, so Kayla headed to the bus stop to wait on the bus to take her home. Her home girl Hope stayed with her while she waited. Not even a minute arriving at the stop, Jackson rolled by in his Chevy Malibu bumping Scarface fuck faces.

He turned the music down a bit, "Where you going?" he asked.

"Home," Kayla responded.

"You want a ride?"

"Yes, I do," Kayla said. She told Hope thank you and said bye. Hope reminded her to be careful, looking out like a friend should. Then Kayla hopped in the car and rode off with Jackson. Jackson asked her where she stayed then turned back up the music and headed that way. As they got closer to her neighborhood he suddenly took a detour.

"I got to stop by my house and get something," he said. Kayla nodded okay. They pulled up to a house not too far from Kim's.

"This is my sister's house. I stay here with her," he said. Then he said, "Aye come in real quick while I grab something." Kayla got out and followed him inside the house. Jackson didn't need to grab anything he was trying to hit, but he played it off. Kayla figured that's what he was up to but she played along. He gave her a semi tour and then showed her his room.

"This is my room," he said, as he flicked the light on then right back off. He grabbed Kayla by the waist and turned her around. They kissed and soon their clothes where on the floor and so where they. Kayla ended up on top of him. He guided her onto his dick and kept his hands on her waist as she began to slowly go up and down on him. At first Kayla was shy and awkward, but the reaction she got from Jackson threw the shyness out the window. After a few minutes, Jackson took control and turned her over to hit it from the back. That position didn't last long, because he quickly came.

Both of them where silent as they got dressed. Jackson got a couple of washrags and they cleaned up. The ride home was awkward. The next words that were spoken between them were "Thank you," from Kayla when they pulled up to Kim's house, and "Alright," from him as a response.

Kayla's mind was all messed up. Things with Jackson only started out of revenge but, after having sex she felt differently. She liked him, but she didn't know how he felt. She kept her feelings to herself and she barely hit him up or even acknowledged him when she saw him in the hood. Outside of a "What's up?" the conversation was always minimal.

— 10 —

RULES, WHAT RULES?

Although living with Kim was all good, Kayla was used to living a certain type of life. For years, she had fended for herself and looked out for herself. She was just a young teen but she was stuck in her ways of doing things. She did what she wanted to do when she wanted to do it. Rules were hard to follow and that was a challenge for Kim who wanted to look out for the girl, and love and care for her as if she was her own. Kim was young herself and didn't quite know how to do that, but she was trying her hardest to make it happen.

After a while, Kim got back with her ex-boyfriend Richard. Richard would always have his homies over kicking it, smoking, drinking, playing video games, which didn't help her situation with Kayla at all. Kim often stayed in her room when he had his company, and Kayla took advantage of that, finding her way down the stairs to join the party. Richard had no problem allowing her to partake in the festivities, he even paid her in weed to iron his clothes for him. Kim knew this was going on, but she didn't say anything to Richard about it. That was mostly because she feared him. Richard was obviously in control of Kim.

Richard began using Kim's car leaving her at home. He picked up Kayla up from school which was something that Kim usually did. One day instead of taking her directly home, he made a pit stop in Tommy Rose apartments. Kayla went inside with him and it turned out to be Cynthia's apartment, one of Michael's ex-girlfriends. It was obvious that Cynthia and Ricky were messing around because they greeted each other with a hug and a kiss. He did that right in front of Kayla like he didn't care. Kayla was shocked, but she didn't say anything about it because Richard supplied her with weed and always allowed her to hang out and kick it regardless of Kim's wishes. He was cool with her.

~

Kim had let a lot of things slide with Kayla. She had only put her on punishment twice, although she probably deserved to be on a punishment way more for all the stuff she had done. Kayla was the sneak out queen, and the majority of the time she had gotten away with it. Except for when her friend Shakina stayed over, when Kayla snuck out the house to hang with her friend Larry and left Shakina in the room asleep.

Larry was a hustler that used to attend North High, but he dropped out and had succumbed to the street life. However, he still came up to the school every day to see his home boys still going to school, and to holler at the girls. Kayla met him through some associates at North. He used to buy the clothes they boosted. He would often be their transportation to and from the mall.

Larry was tall, skinny, and dark skin. He had a brush cut and was well groomed and always smelled good. He drove a Camaro which was freshly painted gray, with some 20-inch rims, and he had that slump.

When he tried to holler at Kayla he didn't have to try too hard—he was flashy and fine. He always kept weed on deck and had no problem sharing. That was right up Kayla's alley.

A fine nigga with a car, and kept a bag of weed that he didn't mind sharing. Shakina was going out with his home boy Rob. They lived in the same hood so, all four of them used to hang out together.

Larry actually had a girlfriend at the time. She went to Central, and was the same age as Kayla. Kayla actually knew the girl. Her name was Cora, and she and Kayla actually used to be cool. They both had attended McMillan Junior High, and started their high school journey off at Central together until Kayla transferred to Benson.

Kayla knew Cora and they had no issues with each other, but that wasn't going to stop Kayla from messing around with her boyfriend. Kayla figured she didn't owe her any loyalty. Larry was young, fine, and paid--and she currently had his attention. Kayla figured it is what it is, Cora may have been his girlfriend but he was Kayla's boo too. It seemed as if he was more interested in spending his time with Kayla anyway. Every chance he had he was picking her up to ride and smoke, or calling her on the phone.

Even on Larry's birthday he chose Kayla over Cora. Kayla, Shakina, and Larry were sitting in the car in front of Kim's house smoking and listening to Trick Daddy featuring Trina "You don't know nan'n." Kayla and Shakina were rapping along with Trina's lyrics, and Larry was rapping to Trick's lyrics. They were straight kicking it, getting high, having a good time together. Then his phone rang, "shhh, be quiet," he said putting his finger over his mouth and turning down the music.

"Hello" his said answering the phone.

"What you doing" Cora asked. The car was so quiet that Kayla and Shakina could hear every word he said like she was on the speaker phone.

"You coming over tonight," she asked him.

"I don't think so," he replied.

"Why?" They could hear the disappointment in her voice when she asked him why.

"I'm busy" he lied.

Well he was sort of busy entertaining Kayla, who was rubbing and kissing all on him the whole time he was on the phone. He could hardly concentrate on his conversation with Cora. He kept saying "Huh?" "What?" Over and over again.

Cora was irritated with him, "What are you doing," she asked several times throughout the conversation.

Of course he kept lying to her saying, "Nothing, just chilling."

"I'm going to call you back," he told her tired of repeating himself as she kept inquiring why he wasn't coming over to her house that night. He was anxious to get her off the phone, and get back to what he was doing. When he hung up they turned the music back on and continued smoking and jamming to the music. Larry had put his girlfriend on the back burner in order to spend his birthday night with Kayla. This girl was something different, and he had been spending a lot of time to get to the point where he could fuck her. His birthday was that night—it was like her gift to him.

After they got done smoking a few blunts, Larry left, but before he left he told Kayla "Aye, make sure you answer that phone later."

She smiled and said "I will," smiling seductively as she walked away. Kayla and Shakina laughed their asses off as they talked about the conversation he had with his girlfriend.

"Girl, he told her ass straight no," Shakina said. Kayla laughed they thought that was cute.

Later on, Larry called, ready for her to come over to his house. Everyone was asleep, including Shakina. So Kayla got up, grabbed her keys and snuck out the back door.

Larry was parked a few doors down waiting for her. It took her a few minutes trying to be quiet and sneak out that back door without being caught, but he was patient. She jumped in the car and he sparked the blunt he had rolled for them to smoke. He also passed her the bottle of Hennessey that he had just cracked open. Kayla took a few swigs and passed it back to him. Drinking really wasn't her thing, because she had many bad experiences with alcohol and she didn't want to have one with him. So they rode around getting high and tipsy, listening to a new Trick Daddy CD.

They pulled up to his house off the deuce four, and he played track #10 off the CD—"I'll be your other man." Then he took his shot and leaned over for a kiss. Kayla climbed over the seat and straddled his lap. They continued to kiss she could feel his dick getting hard as she kissed him and grinded her pelvis on to him. They started off in the car but that quickly got uncomfortable. So he took her in the house. They didn't even make it upstairs to his bedroom, they had sex right on the living room floor. Afterwards they both fell asleep, until about 5 in the morning when they woke up to footsteps upstairs. It was his mom getting up for the day.

"Aw shit, my momma!" They both jumped up and flew out the back door. Neither one of them were fully dressed, but half of her clothes were still in the car anyway.

Kayla had snuck out and was out acting all grown, but back home some trouble was about to happen. A little while after she left, Shakina's boyfriend had called on Kayla's teenline and Shakina made plans to get picked up. Shakina left noisily out the front door. The noise woke Kim up and she saw Shakina leave, so Kim went upstairs to Kayla's room to inquire about her friend leaving in the middle of the night. That's when she discovered Kayla was gone.

When Kayla returned early in the morning sneaking back in through the back door and up to her room, she was greeted with a note from Kim on her bed. The note was letting her know that she did not appreciate her sneaking out of the house and that she was on a punishment. Kim had also taken her phone out of the room. If it wasn't for Shakina being careless, Kayla would never have been caught. She had snuck out the house many times before and had never been caught. Kayla accepted her punishment which really wasn't a big deal to have her phone being taken away. Kim never knew that every time she left, Kayla retrieved her phone that was hidden in Kim's room closet and made her calls, and she just put it back before Kim returned home.

After that night, and once she got off punishment Kayla and Larry started spending a lot of time together. It was like Kayla was his girlfriend rather than his actual girlfriend. Larry had Kayla sneaking off doing shit she had never done before. She wasn't innocent before, but now she was doing way more than she had ever done before trying to be with a nigga.

She'd steal clothes from the mall for him sometimes for free or for the low. She was often skipping school to be with him all day. Kayla's friend Shakina was going out with one of his homies from the hood, so they all ended up hanging out all the time. Kayla and Shakina together were a force to be reckoned with. Kayla would use her as an excuse to get out the house and vice versa. They were always out and about getting into something together.

The two girls snuck off to the hotel with Larry and Anthony one night. It wasn't any fancy hotel like the Holiday Inn or Comfort Inn, it was the Econo Lodge downtown. Econo wasn't nothing but a hole-in-the-wall half-ass excuse for a hotel. Mostly drug deals and prostitution went on inside.

Kayla had been to that hotel/motel before. Back when she was running the streets from here to there with her momma. Kay's ex John Smith had rented a room quite a few times when he was homeless and bumming around. Kay, being in love, followed right behind him, and dragged Kayla right with her. None of them were old enough to rent a room themselves. So they had to recruit a crack head to do the dirty work for them. For a piece of rock it wasn't a hard task. It didn't matter to the girls as long as they could spend time with them niggas getting high, drunk and kicking it.

That night Kayla showed Larry her loyalty to him and just how down she was for him by holding his crack package in her vagina for him as he sat outside the hotel hustling. Once his pack was gone they went up to the room with Kina and Anthony. The night was wild and crazy everybody was drunk and high. None of them had a care in the world. Larry and Kayla had one bed and Shakina and Anthony had the other. It was going down in that room. The dude tried to be slick thinking that they were about to switch girls and some more shit, but their plan didn't work.

"Aye, I bet you the pussy better over here," one said, then the other repeated the statement. Then Kina and Anthony hopped in the same bed as Kayla and Larry, but neither one of the girls was with the shit they were trying to pull at all. So they left well enough alone and Kina and Anthony jumped back to their own bed.

Then there was a knock at the door. It just so happened to be Kayla's older cousin on her father's side. She was strung out on crack and happened to be one of the dudes' clients. She immediately recognized her cousin who was Who was being grown laid up in a hotel room with a nigga. None of that mattered to her cousin—she had one mission and one mission only, and that was to get high. That crack was a motherfucka because none of that mattered to her—she was on a mission of her own. She could not have cared less about what was going on, because she was too busy chasing another type of high.

"Aye, I got this liquor, do y'all want to buy it?" she asked.

Larry brought the liquor off of her. Kayla just wanted her cousin up and out of there, and figuring that if they brought the weed it was less likely that she'd tell Ray what she had just witnessed.

— 11 —

NEW HOOD

Near the end of 1998 and the beginning of 1999 everybody slowly started moving out of the projects to 48th Street at n apartment area off of Ames. The 48 was just like the projects. The girls quickly adjusted to the different setting. Just like in Spencer, a lot of their family and friends lived up between Sahler and Taylor blocks. Renay and their Aunt Darla, Tracy, and the home girl Tish all lived on Sahler Street in different apartment buildings, Then Trina stayed on Taylor Street in some apartments. They were deep up there just like they used to be down in Spencer. It didn't take long for them to get to know the other people in the neighborhood. Everywhere they went, they fit right in like they had been around their whole lives.

Kim was very lenient on Kayla and barely punished her for anything, but a few times she was forced to put her foot down. The second time she had to punish her was when Kayla's cousin Jackie randomly decided to play the concerned big cousin and snitch her about not being where she said she was. Kayla had made plans to hang out with Raheem, a dude she met at the mall when she was stealing with her friends.

He wanted her to spend the night with him at his aunt's crib where he was staying. So Kayla made plans to stay the night on the 48 at the home girl Tish's house. She knew Kim wouldn't have a problem with her staying the night over there. She had met Tish before, and Kayla hung out up there on the 48 often with her cousins. Plus a couple of her cousins and an aunt stayed up there in that area as well. So Kayla packed her overnight bag and Kim dropped her off. Raheem had picked her up once Kim was gone.

Kayla and Rah had been talking every day since they had met; he even came to Kim's house to chill with Kayla a few times. They sat outside on the stairs and got to know each other. After talking every day for weeks, they decided it was time to take their relationship to the next level. That night, they arrived at Rah's spot and he made her feel welcomed and comfortable. He cooked dinner of steak, shrimp, and baked potatoes. He was really into her. After they ate, he poured her some Asti that he bought because she told him that it was her favorite drink.

After dinner, he started to give her a massage. The massage was not only turning her on, but he was getting turned on as well. So he invited her into his bedroom. Kayla was a little nervous, but she followed his lead. She had made a mix tape especially for that occasion so she pulled it out of her purse and gave it to him. He popped it in and as soon as the music started to play, so did they. Rah hit the lights and laid her on the bed and removed all her clothes and then his too.

Kayla wasn't a virgin, but everything about her experience with Rah was different. He was taking his time, paying attention to Kayla and her body. She hadn't experienced any of that with her previous partners. Rah was extremely well endowed and she was intimidated by that at first, but he took his time and instead of the pain she anticipated, it was pleasure as he inserted every inch of his manhood inside of her. They made love to the whole mix tape front and back, and when the music stopped he flipped the tape and they went at it again to the music front and back. His stroke matched every beat and lyric to the music. After they fucked to the tape front and back twice it had finally come to an end. They both were exhausted, so they just laid there still and speechless. "I have to go to the bathroom" Kayla finally said after about ten minutes breaking the silence in the room.

Rah hopped up to allow her to get up off of the bed. She attempted to stand, but her legs were so weak she fell back onto the bed. Rah let out a giggle. That boosted his ego—it confirmed that he had put in work. In a few minutes, she was able to get up and go to the bathroom. They showered together. He washed her body and she washed his, and they shared several intimate kisses. Then they lay in the bed together naked and passed out in each other's arms.

Kayla woke up the following day and was mesmerized; she didn't want her time with Rah to end. It was like a dream. That morning they fucked again then shared another shower and got ready for the day. Rah was something different. He put lotion on Kayla's body, and even ironed her clothes for her. Then they headed to the homegirl Tish's house, where she was supposed to have been the whole time. He came in and met her friend and hung out for a few hours. Tish got to know him a little and they played cards and just talked. Once he left Tish was all happy for Kayla.

"Girl, where did you meet him?" she asked. She was amazed at how he represented himself, and she could tell that he was really into her friend. Shortly after he left, Jackie came through the door. Kayla thought she could share her story with Jackie, but that was a mistake. She didn't get the response that she was looking for.

"You spent the night with who?" Jackie questioned angrily. That caught everybody off guard. Jackie was famous for switching up her attitude. One minute she was your BFF, the next she was this concerned adult.

"Aww hell to the NO, what in the fuck? You're lucky that I wasn't here when he was I would have let that nigga have it," she went on with a look on her face to let everyone know that she was dead ass serious.

Tish tried to intervene, "But I met him and he seems nice and cool, and he's really into her," she said trying to calm Jackie down and attempting to make the situation better.

Jackie wasn't hearing it. "It doesn't matter, she's not grown, and she had no business spending the night with this nigga." Then she turned to Tish, "And you are wrong for allowing the nigga to sit up here in your house with her."

Tish just looked stunned, "I'm sorry," she said and then didn't say another word.

Jackie was going off, she went on and on about it. Kayla was annoyed, because Jackie didn't have a problem with smoking weed and cigarettes, or drinking with her, but she had a problem with her spending the night with a dude. Jackie went on and on sounding like a broken record chastising Kayla and Tish. Her words were going in one ear and out the other. The only person she may have been scaring was Tish because Kayla clearly didn't give a fuck. Tish started repeatedly apologizing while Kayla let Jackie's words right pass on by.

She was so sometimey. Just like when she made Kayla tell Michael her real age because she was too young for him, but that very same night she snuck her out of the house to go smoke Michael's weed, and allowed Kayla to be hugged up kissing on him. Jackie was a walking contradiction. One minute Kayla was old enough to hang with and allowed her to participate in all kinds of other illegal inappropriate shit that a minor shouldn't be doing, and the next she treated Kayla as a child. It made absolutely no sense what so ever.

Jackie wasn't done after the complete cuss out—she wasn't satisfied. She took things a step further and called Kim to inform her of everything. She also added on the information about Kayla skipping school. A few weeks prior on her way to work, she saw Kayla on the bus.

"Kayla, what are you doing," she said as she saw her cousin boarding the number 18 bus on 36th Ames right outside of North High School.

"School got out early," Kayla tried to lie, caught off guard.

Jackie knew she was lying, because it was early in the morning and school had barely gotten started so there was no way it was out already. Jackie hadn't told on Kayla immediately but apparently, she felt the need to add that information as she told on Kayla's night with Rah.

So that marked the second time Kim put Kayla on a punishment. She shortened her weekend and came to pick her up. To make matters worse, shortly after Kayla arrived home, she was in her room. Then there was a knock on her room door, when it opened it was Jackie and Keisha. Kayla rolled her eyes at the sight of her cousin. Apparently she felt she hadn't done enough, and came over to rub it in. Jackie was the last person that Kayla wanted to see…

"I know you mad at me right, now, but I love you and I told for your own good."

Kayla gave Jackie a deadly look but didn't say a word.

"I love you anyway, give me a hug," she went on.

She thought to herself, "Yeah right." Jackie had her fucked up; she didn't even understand why she was even there. All Kayla heard was blah, blah, blah. She wasn't giving her a hug and she wasn't interested in seeing or hearing her..

"You'll appreciate me one day," Jackie said before leaving, but Kayla could care less what she was talking about.

～

The final straw came Kayla got suspended from school for "fighting." That time really wasn't Kayla's fault, but the fact that she was suspended from school seemed to be the only thing Kim was concerned about. About a month before Kayla was suspended from school, Kayla had gotten into an argument with a girl that was in her math class. The girl bumped into Kayla after class one day as she was playing around with one of the male students.

Irritated, Kayla said "excuse you" to the girl who didn't even bother to say sorry.

The girl didn't like her tone so she said, "You don't have to have an attitude, bitch."

Kayla snapped back and said, "Bitch!" The two passed more words back and forth, but they didn't fight.

Besides shooting each other nasty looks when they were in each other's presence, nothing came from their argument. About a month later, the other girl was ready to address the issue. Right before class, both girls were in a bathroom at the same time. Brandi left out first, she turned and looked at Kayla as if she had something to say, but she didn't say a word—she just walked out of the bathroom. Kayla had prepared herself to respond to the girl, but when she didn't say anything Kayla just washed her hands and went to her classroom waiting for her class to start.

The teacher had recently changed the seating chart and Kayla was sitting in the middle row of the class in the front seat. Brandi sat to the right in the back row. Right before the bell rang Kayla felt a yank at her ponytail, and was attacked with punches to her head from the back. Before she knew what was going on Brandi was getting the best of her. She tried to stand and fight back, but by the time she did, the teacher and security had made it into the room to break it up.

"Now bitch, talk shit" is all she could hear the girl say.

Kayla was pissed and embarrassed now. "Bitch why you wait until I was off guard? I said bitch, why you wait til I was off guard to sucker punch me?"

Kayla received a five-day suspension even though she didn't even get a lick in. None of that mattered to the Administrator. Two girls fighting was all he saw.

When the weekend came, Kayla asked if she could go to the mall with her cousin Avery.

"I wouldn't feel right letting you go to the mall being suspended from school," Kim said.

Kayla tried to argue her point, but Kim wouldn't hear it. Kayla was pissed off. How was she being punished for getting jumped on? For once she truly had done nothing wrong, but that didn't matter. The school didn't care and her guardian didn't care. It was bullshit. So she went to her room pissed. She started writing a letter to her cousin Avery expressing how she felt about the whole situation. That was a tradition/ritual they created at her Aunt Lynn's house. Not only did Kayla express how she felt about that situation, but she started talking about how dumb Kim was, how Ricky was dogging her and treating her, and how she just accepted it.

After venting in her letter Kayla decided that she was going to the mall with her cousin with or without Kim's permission, and she did just that. Kim had some errands to run, so she just left and told Kayla she'd be back. Kayla did an old school trick an put some pillows under her blanket to make it seem as if she was asleep and she left the house.

While Kim was out running errands, she thought a lot about the situation and had come to the conclusion that Kayla was truly not at fault in this fight. She had decided to let Kayla go to the mall. When she came home, she called call Kayla to the kitchen. No answer. Kim called a few more times and still did not get an answer, so she went to Kayla's room check on her. She figured the teen was ignoring her because she was mad, but Kayla was gone, Kim quickly noticed the propped up pillows that were meant to trick her, and that made her angry.

As she turned around to leave the room, she noticed the notebook laying open on the bed. She picked it up and read the letter Kayla had started writing to her cousin. Tears fell as she read the harsh words Kayla, a 15 year old girl she had taken in, was saying about her. The words were mostly true, but to read these things about herself and to know that's how Kayla felt hurt her soul.

After reading the letter Kim decided that she was done. Kayla couldn't stay with her anymore, she needed to wash her hands of the situation.

Now Kayla was on the run again. Her caseworker, Joe, tried for weeks to track her down. He found her on the 48 at Tish's house. She didn't want to stay with Tish or any of her other relatives that stayed up there, but she used them all as resources while she was basically homeless.

Every day, Kayla still got up and went to school. For the first week it was like she was in the clear because she'd make it through the whole school day without anyone looking for her. The second week, a police officer came to get her out of class every day for four days straight. They'd remove her from school and take her to what was supposed to be her temporary placement. Kayla wasn't having it she'd play along just long enough for the worker to leave and it never failed once he left so did she. She didn't know if the people were nice or what, and she wasn't willing to give them a chance.

Considering that placing Kayla with her own family wasn't really an option. Joe didn't have many options. He finally sat her down and explained to Kayla that if she ran again, he'd be forced to place her in a locked facility. Kayla realized that she really didn't have a choice but to try to make her next placement work out. She reluctantly agreed.

When she arrived, she was greeted by a middle-aged woman who actually seemed nice. She stayed in a house off of 50th and Center in a good neighborhood.

"Hi I'm Wanda," the woman said extending her hand.

Kayla spoke back softly, as she was extremely sad about her situation. "Hi." She couldn't understand why she had to go through all these changes.

Wanda gave Kayla a heartfelt hug, "It is okay, I understand everything is going to be alright," she said trying to comfort Kayla. She then introduced her to her daughter and her other foster daughter. To Kayla's surprise, she knew the foster daughter. Diamond used to stay next door to her aunt Lynn in the Spencer projects. Her mom Miss Hadley was very strict on her and her sibling. Kayla was shocked to see Diamond in a foster home, but her mother's strictness had been rough on her. She started to rebel against the rules, and the environment became hostile. After the meet and greet, Kayla was shown her room which was in the basement. It was actually nice down there, and she thought she would be very comfortable. At first she wasn't too happy about the way things were happening, but she figured that she would manage. Wanda seemed nice enough, her house was decent, and Kayla knew Diamond.

Kayla started to sense that Wanda was a little different from the jump. The first day she told Kayla, "Oh fix whatever you want to eat. Most of the time we fend for ourselves around here. The next time I go grocery shopping, you can give me a list of some things you like."

That sounded reasonable, so Kayla cooked up some fried chicken and French fries. Kayla had had a long day, and she was hungry. The moment she fixed her plate, Wanda came in the kitchen hovering over Kayla's.

"Mmm that smells so good, can I have it?"

Kayla was shocked and wanted to say no, but she said yes because she felt obligated.

"Mom, that's wrong—don't eat her food," her daughter said. That didn't discourage Wanda at all.

"Well she said I can have it," as she had a seat and devoured the food. Kayla fixed a sandwich instead of the food she just slaved in the kitchen to prepare, since everyone had to fend for themselves. Although Wanda's behavior irritated Kayla a bit, she let that go. That was only the beginning . Wanda had a unique set of house rules, and some unrealistic expectations.

Then the first day Kayla went back to school, Wanda gave her 40 cents. "My daughter usually likes to get an extra milk at lunch, so here you go," she said, handing Kayla a quarter, nickel, and dime,

Kayla took the change, but was thinking "what am I supposed to do with this?" I don't even like milk. She could at least have given her a dollar bill so she could have brought a juice, a cookie or something.

The day Kayla arrived at Wanda's her cousins Avery, Jackie, and Keisha had come by to visit and to help her settle in. Kayla had forgiven Jackie for snitching on her, and they were back tight like sisters. When the girls came over Kayla broke down all over again. "I don't want to stay here," she cried. They cried with their cousin. None of them had the power to change her situation. If they could have they would have in a heartbeat.

Lynn was now staying back with her mom, and there was no way she was going to let Kayla come back to stay. Avery was staying with her mom with her baby. Marie had already tried to take Kayla in before, and it didn't work out. All they could do was hold on to her and attempt to give her words of comfort.

"It's going to be alright, Kayla. We will visit you whenever we can, and you will still be able to come hang with us on the weekend. Look at it like this: in two years you'll be out of school and able to do what you want." They tried to encourage her but it wasn't really working. Two years was a long time. Eventually they got her to calm down. They left her a few cigarettes on the sneak to help ease the pain, and promised to come back soon.

Over the weeks, Kayla started to open up a little more. She gave Wanda a look into her life, where aches had been and what she had been through. Wanda seemed very interested, and acted as if she wanted to help. She had Kayla write down her thoughts and how she felt about her mom. She stated that she wanted to help start a program to bring families back together and wanted to start with Kayla and her mom. Since

Kayla had expressed a desire to mend her broken relationship with her mother, Wanda asked Joe to try to get Kayla to Minnesota to visit her mom. Kayla appreciated that and was open to that possibility. She hadn't seen her mother since the day before she was released from ST. Joseph Mental Hospital and Kayla was moved in to her Aunt Anne's house. Kayla hadn't really expressed it to anyone before, but she resented Kay for that. She felt like her mom just took off and left her daughter, and didn't look back.

A few days went by at Wanda's, and it wasn't horrible. Kayla was getting the gist of things. She stayed in her room listening to music, and she and Diamond talked. Wanda played no games when it came to the showers—she expected showers to be 3 minutes, in and out. That was something Kayla wasn't used to at all and she didn't like it. She liked to get in the shower and relax, but she wasn't able to do that here. It wasn't a deal breaker.

She had also enjoyed watching Comic View on BET for years. Wanda put a stop to that too."I don't think that show is appropriate you shouldn't be watching that". Kayla was annoyed, considering she wasn't a baby and she had been watching that show for as long as she could remember. This rule was something else she had to get used to.

So at first, there were some things that she didn't like, but she was willing to deal with them.

Soon though, Kayla started acting out, and rebelling against Wanda's rules. It was just too much for her to handle. For so long she had been doing what she wanted to do, when and how she wanted to do it. That's why she had a hard time adjusting to anyone's house rules. She was already stuck in her ways and there wasn't any turning her around. Wanda would nitpick at anything and everything that she did. She felt like she couldn't do anything right.

Kayla was still doing some things she shouldn't have been, like smoking cigarettes and smoking them in Wanda's house. She almost got busted a few times and then Wanda flipped when she discovered Kayla had removed the smoke detector battery in the basement. It seemed as if every day Wanda had some new rule or expectation.

Kayla felt locked up, she couldn't smoke her cigarettes like she needed because she was addicted. She couldn't watch the shows she wanted to watch on TV. The weekends took forever to come so she could escape from the shenanigans. She couldn't take the pressure—it was all too much.

Wanda's rules and expectations were virtually impossible to get used to. Wanda had tested her patience, and Kayla had tested hers as well. Finally, Kayla decided she wasn't holding her tongue or playing nice anymore—she was going to tell Wanda about herself.

She didn't cuss Wanda out day one when she ate her food after she spent all that damn time cooking it. She didn't cuss her out after she stopped her from watching her favorite show, Comic view. Kayla had held everything in, because she knew she didn't have any other options.

However, one day, everything came to a boiling point. Wanda was chastising her about skipping school and she informed Kayla that she wouldn't be going anywhere that weekend. Wanda was right —Kayla shouldn't be allowed to go anywhere that weekend. Letting her go would have been like rewarding her for negative behavior. Kayla knew she was in the wrong, but she didn't care about that. Kayla lived for her weekends to get away from Wanda, the rules, and her house. So, she wasn't the least bit happy with this punishment.

"Fuck, you, your daughter, and your house, bitch. I'm gone, and I don't want to stay here anymore anyway," Kayla cursed Wanda and her daughter out and dared somebody to do or say something about it. Wanda was a boujee bitch who acted as if her shit didn't stink. She held Kayla up to unrealistic standards, and then took every chance she could to compare her to her own daughter.

Wanda's daughter wasn't the angel she wanted to believe that she was either. One day her son and daughter gave Kaya a ride to 48th street and her "angel" was getting high, bumping DMX (Flesh of My Flesh, Blood of My Blood) along the way, quoting the lyrics the whole way.

Kayla packed whatever she could stuff into her book bag, and took off on foot. Her destination was to the 48. She was so angry she didn't care about how far the walk was, and the voice of her grandfather was in her head saying, "Walking ain't crowded," fueled her energy and motivated her to keep stepping. After fifteen minutes of walking, her legs burned and her pace slowed. She sat down to take a break at a park. There were some guys playing basketball. She watched them play as she rested her legs.

One of the guys came over to her after the game. "Hey little momma, how are you," he asked as he checked her up and down.

"I'm fine," Kayla replied.

"You need a ride?" Kayla accepted hesitantly because she still had a long way to go before she reached her destination. He was a gentleman and honestly just wanted to offer her a ride and nothing else. That was surprising to Kayla, because almost every man that she knew expected that if he did something for her, he damn sure wanted something in return.

— *12* —

RAY FINALLY TO THE RESCUE

Kayla had no options, she knew before she left Wanda's that if she was caught this time, she would probably be headed to a locked facility due to her history of running.

Ray was currently living in Myatt Apartments with his young girlfriend, Mecca, and her two sons. She was going to be moving into a house soon, and she had extra room for Kayla to stay. So, she did a favor for her man and agreed to let Kayla come live with them.

Ray took Kayla to Wanda's house to retrieve her belongings. Wanda came to the door and said, "Y'all can come in to get her stuff, but Kayla will need to apologize to me before she is welcome to come in"

Ray looked at Kayla, for a response and Kayla looked right back at Wanda and then back at Ray. "I'll just wait in the car" she said. If looks could kill, Wanda would be deceased. There was no way that Kayla was going to apologize to Wanda, so she shrugged her shoulders and went to the car to wait. She was not sorry and was not going to pretend to be sorry, either. So Ray had to go inside and retrieve Kayla's belongings himself.

For the first few nights Kayla had to bunk in with Mecca's boys. She was happy to be in a comfortable bed. Soon after

Kayla moved in with her dad and his girlfriend, they moved into a house. Kayla was given the basement where she had a pull-out couch to sleep on, and her own private space. She was happy with that. The school year was almost over and summer was approaching. Mecca seemed cool, so Kayla was pretty comfortable staying there with them. Things started off good—Mecca took her shopping and made her feel comfortable in her home.

Mecca had never imagined playing the role of stepmom to Ray's daughter. She was only in her mid-twenties, and her kids were younger... and boys. She had no idea what to do with a teenage girl. She had only interacted with Kayla twice prior to her coming to live with them. Once Ray had picked Mecca up to have lunch with him and Kayla. It was not a good interaction, because Kayla acted like a spoiled brat and would not get out of the front seat. Ultimately, Mecca didn't join them on the lunch date.

The second interaction was when Kayla knocked on her door in Myatt's asking to buy a twenty bag of weed. She didn't sell it to her. She opened her door, shocked to see Ray's daughter who she recognized immediately even though she had only met her once. "Mecca didn't waste any time telling Ray about the incident. Mecca did a lot of that telling once Kayla moved in. She told Ray about every move she witnessed Kayla make.

～

During the summer, Kayla was allowed to live the life she had been living before, pretty much. Her dad allowed her to continue to go hang out on 48th Street and down in Spencer projects. Kayla even got a part time job at a telemarketing company where her cousin Jackie worked.

As summer ended and her junior year was about to begin, Kayla was back to her normal kicking it down in Spencer and up on the 48th Street. The 48 had become the main hangout spot, since everyone she knew had moved up there. Kayla's cousin Renee, T, and her aunt Darla, and their homegirls, Tish and Trina, all lived up there between the Taylor and Sahler blocks. Like anywhere else they went, they quickly got to know the people in the neighborhood.

Kayla met a young dude named Johnny—everyone called him J.J. He was light skinned and fine. Kayla wasted no time at all getting to know him. He stayed with his mom and his two sisters who were part of a popular local dance group. Every morning that Kayla stayed the night on the 48 she would go to their apartment and wake him up to come outside and chill with her. He never hesitated and they quickly built a friendship—but that's all it was for a long time. J.J. liked Kayla but she was too busy smiling up in the faces of all the other hustler thug-type niggas on the block. Besides, Kayla had her eyes on a guy named Doug who lived in the upstairs apartment right above Tish. He was in his twenties—way too old for Kayla, and he had a girlfriend with a son and a baby on the way. None of that mattered to Kayla; he was fine, and he was the weed man. He always came outside and smoked with Kayla and her homegirl, and he obviously had an interest in her. Kayla naturally had lied about her age knowing if he knew her true age he wouldn't even be entertaining her.

Every day on 48th Street was a kick-it session. There was an older cat named Bo who had recently moved to Omaha from California. He hung with nothing but young cats. He could easily influence them and they all followed him just like they were playing follow the leader. Bo was crazy and didn't need no fucking with—especially when he was drinking. He was real cool, but at the same damn time he was crazy.

Kayla and Keisha witnessed him get drunk and beat up one of the young dudes like he wasn't shit. However crazy or not, he had the turn-up spot and everybody kept going over there to get drunk and high for free.

Kayla was gone from home as much as possible. Whenever she was home, she stayed in the basement to herself talking on the phone. A person would have thought that she and Ray would have become closer, but it was the total opposite. Kayla didn't even feel as if that was her home. She didn't even have a key to the house.

Even when Christmas came Kayla didn't feel included. She waited for someone to come wake her, but they never did. She lay on her pull out bed and listed as Mecca's boys opened their gifts in excitement. As Mecca and her dad watched. When she did get up, she had no audience. She just opened her few items silently by herself.

— 13 —

LONG TIME NO SEE

Crazy ass Wanda was good for one idea—she wanted to visit her mom Kay in Minnesota. It had been a few years since Kayla had seen her and she missed her mother, regardless of all they had been through. The state of Nebraska was willing to pick up the trip all-expenses paid, so Jackie contacted Kayla's caseworker, Joe, to put the plan into action for them to take the trip. Kay was in prison serving a two-year sentence she had received due to domestic violence case she had with Lewis. Minnesota didn't play around—they handed out jail time like nobody's business. All the craziness she pulled in Nebraska didn't fly in Minnesota. In Nebraska, if the witness didn't show up to court, the state didn't have a case. In Minnesota, it didn't matter if the victim showed up or not.

They decided to turn Kayla's visit into a trip for their whole crew. Getting there seemed like it took forever. With the back seat full it was the longest eight hours of their life. They had brought a half ounce of weed, which was some back yard bunk ass shit. It seemed like no matter how many blunts they smoked they still weren't getting high. They each even rolled up a personal blunt and blazed and still nothing.

When they arrived in Minnesota, they were excited and headed straight to the downtown area to walk around. When they got there, they immediately met some niggas who promised to show them how to get to a nice hotel. So being naïve, they split up and Kayla and Avery rode with the dudes and the other girls followed in their car.

"Oh hell naw," Kayla and Avery said in unison as they pulled up on the motel. Their crew was saying the same thing in the next car. These dudes had really taken them to a motel and there was no way they were going to be staying anytime at all in there. They weren't with it at all.

So the guys said, "Okay, we'll take y'all somewhere else."

This time, Kayla and Avery got out of their car and jumped back in the car with their own crew. They attempted to follow the niggas, but it seemed as if the guys were purposely trying to ditch them on the interstate as fast as they were driving. It was either that or they were just driving fast because Minnesota drivers have a need for speed. So the girls gave up trying to keep up with them and started searching for a room on their own. Unfortunately, their trip was happening while there was a baseball tournament going on, and every last hotel room in the city was booked. After a few hour of no luck finding a room, they decided to get some food.

Soon, they found out that Minnesota had a curfew for minors, so Kayla and Keisha weren't allowed to dine at the restaurants. They found a White Castle restaurant, got take out, and slept in the car in the parking lot of a hotel until people started checking out of the hotel later that morning. Their first few hours of vacation had been pure hell, but that wasn't going to stop them. They were determined to have a good trip.

After hours of being uncomfortable, they got a room and were able to wind down a little, take showers, and prepare Kayla to her visit with Kay. They got directions to the prison from the hotel staff, and off they went.

Kayla and Jackie were the only ones approved to visit, so Avery dropped them off. Kayla was excited to see Kay walk through the doors of the visiting room. She embraced her mom with a hug, and shed a few tears. It had been a long time since she had seen her, and she needed it.

Those two hours passed by quickly. They played cards— Kay taught her daughter and niece how to play a game called "Trash". They laughed at the stories Kay told about her having to check a few inmates in there, and about her jailhouse meals such as burritos and fried noodles. They had a good time, and Kayla didn't want the visit to end, but she knew she could come back the next day.

By the time the visit was over Avery had made some calls and had gotten into contact with some family they had nearby, and also Kay's boyfriend Lewis. Lewis agreed to let them board at his apartment while they were there. So they went back to the hotel to get their things, and Lewis met them there and took them to his apartment. Then they wanted to have some fun.

None of them had ever been to the Mall of America, so that was their first stop. They made a mistake by splitting up and not writing down where they parked. When they were tired of shopping and roaming the mall, it took a few hours to find where they had parked. Kayla and Avery found the car first, but they had to sit inside for a couple hours waiting for the rest of the crew to find them. Then the car wouldn't start.

It seemed like they weren't having any luck on their trip. When they realized that the car wouldn't start due to the car being in gear, they laughed hysterically at the stupidity of the situation and dipped out.

Next thing on their agenda was to find some weed. The bunk weed they came with just wasn't getting it done, and it was raining on their parade.

Somehow they ended up in the hood and just like when they arrived in town, they ran into a couple of niggas. The dudes were brothers and invited them to their house. They were in a group, so they figured it wouldn't be any harm. Also, there were more of them than the dudes, so they went with them and bought some weed and blazed with them. They had a few drinks and laughed and kicked it with them for a few. Their weed wasn't that good either but it was definitely better that what they had come with.

Later, they hooked up with their older cousins, Don and Walt. These guys were crazy—the last time they had seen them they were in Omaha for their father's funeral. That was an unforgettable trip. Don beat up his girl in front of everybody, and put her head in the toilet giving her a swirly. Walt and Don got into it and Walter straight left his brother in Omaha stranded.

This time, they tried to show their little cousins a good time in Minneapolis. The girls wanted to see what Minnesota had to offer, what the night life looked like. However, Kayla and Keisha were too young to do what they wanted. The older girls tried to ditch the girls so they could go clubbing, but Kayla and Keisha weren't having it. They headed back to Lewis's apartment and called it a night.

The following day Kayla and Jackie went to their visit with Kay. That time saying goodbye was hard because that was goodbye for a while. Kayla would be going back to Omaha and Kay still had at least six months left on her sentence. There wasn't any telling when they would see each other again.

— 14 —

JUNIOR YEAR

———————∧———————

Summer was over and Kayla was about the start her Junior Year. It was a new start for her. She was happy with her living situation. It wasn't picture perfect, but at least she was with her dad. His girlfriend was sometimey—one day she was cool and the next day she was snitching on every move Kayla made. She was doing her job as Ray's girl. She was technically Kayla's step-mom now, so she had to play the role and she played the position well.

Kayla had started her high-school journey off at Central, but had transferred to Benson for ninth grade, then she attended North for sophomore year. Now she was back where she had started. Some of the people she started there with were still there and some had also transferred to other schools.

One girl Kayla new back then was Cora, who still went to Central. She and Kayla used to be cool—they both went to McMillan together. She happened to be Larry's girlfriend. Kayla and Larry had messed around for about a year, and Kayla knew about Cora, but Cora didn't know about Kayla.

A few months prior, Kayla and Jackie were at the bank where Cora worked. Kayla tried to tell Jackie secretly that Cora was Larry's girlfriend. Well Jackie was being her normal ghetto self and loudly said "Who Larry?" getting the attention of Cora.

Cora said "Excuse me?"

Jackie went on, "Is your name Larry?"

"No but that's my man," she said with an obvious attitude.

"Oh, really" Jackie said sarcastically then she moved on to the next teller.

Kayla stood there with guilt all over her face and said nothing. She couldn't believe her cousin had caused that scene, but that was Jackie. Just Kayla's luck, she now had a few classed with Cora, which wasn't a surprise considering they both were juniors that year. So due to that incident at the bank, Cora wasn't feeling Kayla, and she didn't even try to hide it when she saw her.

~

Gunter was at Central when Kayla first attended freshman year, and from what she could remember, all the girls talked about him like he was the finest thing walking around. She never really got a chance to meet him since she transferred schools, but she still knew of him thanks to all the girls who were head over heels for him. Even when she attended North her sophomore year he was the talk of the town. Especially from a girl named Nicki that Kayla knew.

"Gunter is my boo, I love him," she would exclaim as she made dreamy eyes.

When Kayla transferred back to Central her junior year, she too became infatuated with Gunter, and then he became her boo. He was tall, caramel colored, and sexy. He wasn't as fine as Kayla expected him to be. He wore his hair in braids and had a slightly receding hairline, but he had sex appeal about him. He also had an amazing personality, he was a very welcoming person and he was funny. Those were the qualities that made him most attractive.

Gunter was a two time senior and should have graduated the year prior, but he was a goof ball and fucked off during some of his time in high school. He and Kayla shared a Foods and Nutrition class together. That's how the two started talking and hanging out. Kayla was hesitant to talk to him at first, because he was friends with another boy she had been talking to, Kirk. Apparently they were from the same hood, but Gunter wasn't backing down. He was interested in Kayla, and he was going to get at her one way or another regardless who she was talking to.

Larry's girlfriend, Cora, was also in that same class and she did not like Kayla. She tried hard to make Kayla jealous when it came to Gunter. She'd always call him her husband in class making sure Kayla heard her calling him that. Her plan backfired because he wasn't interested in her like that. Plus, he was too busy trying to get with Kayla at the time. Kayla thought Cora was funny and paid her no attention what so ever. She had Gunter's attention, and little did Cora know, she still had Larry's attention too.

After a few weeks, Gunter convinced Kayla to come chill with him at his house. He had early outs she didn't but she left early with him anyway. They caught the bus to his house and chilled out. She met his mom who was surprisingly extremely cool. He tried to fuck her that day, but she liked him, so she held back on giving him any.

The next time they hung out though, she gave in and she then knew what all the hype was about. She was officially in a trance and couldn't stay away from him.

Kayla stopped hanging on the 48 as much because all the free time she had she spent with him. When she got out of school she went to his house, when she got off work she was there. It got to where she started getting phone calls at his house.

Spending so much time with Gunter, she almost lost her boo, John, because she had stopped hanging out on the 48. She heard Jackie and Keisha went to the movies with Bo and JJ. She wasn't having that—she had put months into JJ. He belonged to her even though they hadn't done anything yet. Once she found about the so-called movie date she had to make her presence known.

She took a break from Gunter and went to see what was up with JJ. To avoid any misunderstandings after six months of playing games, flirting, and talking on the phone Kayla gave JJ some. JJ wasn't ready but, at the same time he was ready. Kayla caught him off guard. He was starting to think that she wasn't interested any more. Kayla took him to the back room at Bo's house and took control.

Kayla was far from a virgin and had some experience, but she was used to being submissive. With JJ she had to take control. He talked a good game but when it came to action he seemed to not know what to do. Kayla assumed he was a virgin by his actions. He didn't have any sense of direction and she had to show him what to do, but he caught on. After that session she had him where she wanted him and had reclaimed her boo.

~

Between attending school, working, and juggling JJ and Gunter, Kayla was trying to do everything. In addition to spending time at home sometimes. Kayla would go see JJ before school on most days. She'd get on the bus and go up to the 48 to kick it with him for a few then get on the bus and go to school.

JJ and Kayla were so cute together. Both of them tried to act as if they weren't fascinated with one another. From the first day they met on 48th Street, they couldn't stay away from each other. Kayla made it a point to go knocking at his apartment door every morning when she stayed the night up there with her cousin. It didn't matter if he was dead tired, he didn't hesitate to get up when she came knocking. His older sisters would tease him about it. They weren't used to him jumping for a girl. Plus, he was their little brother, and it wouldn't be right if they didn't give him a hard time and tease him.

The two built a true friendship and bond. This was a first for Kayla, because up until then most guys she dealt with just wanted to have sex with her. The relationship with JJ was different. They actually talked and got to know one another. When Kayla wasn't on the block, the two would spend countless hours on the phone. They even fell asleep the on the phone with each other. It was like they could never get enough.

Juggling JJ and Gunter got hard for Kayla—she liked both of them. Between school and home, it was hard trying to keep up with the two. Both of them wanted to spend time with her. It was all going well until she got caught up when she accidentally made plans with both boys the same day. So, she went to hang out with JJ first. The plan was to smoke with him, then head to Gunter's house. She spent more time with JJ than expected, and Gunter ended up paging her on her beeper to see where she was.

Her mistake was using the phone where she was at to call him back. On her way to Gunter's, he called the number back and got JJ, which blew up her whole plan. That incident was the end for her and Gunter. He was jealous and pissed off to find out Kayla was lying to him.

Living with Ray and his girlfriend Mecca had its challenges because Mecca was young too, and she and Kayla often bumped heads. Any and every little thing she saw Kayla do, she'd run and tell Ray. She couldn't have company or anything like that. Once Jackie came over to visit and Mecca had a hissy fit. Kayla wasn't even allowed to have a house key. Other than that, Kayla was able to come and go as she pleased. She made sure she came home during the weekdays at a decent hour, but Kayla was always on the go.

One night as she was heading out, she asked Larry to pick her up and Ray pulled up at the same time.

"Who is that nigga?" he questioned his daughter.

She quickly came up with a lie, "That my cousin," knowing damn well that wasn't any of her relatives. Ray knew better as well, but he just gave her a crazy look and let her leave with him.

~

Ray wasn't always on the up and up, and he ended up getting 90 days in jail for driving under a suspended license. During that time Kayla really started doing whatever she wanted. Once Ray was locked up, Mecca became a little more lenient as well. She'd pay Kayla to babysit. She would take Kayla wherever she wanted to go. Maybe it was because she was off doing her own thing as well. Kayla didn't know and she didn't care—she was enjoying how things were going.

— 15 —
EVEN FAMILY WANTS
TO SEE YOU FAIL

"You ain't going to be shit. You going to be just like your momma," Kayla's older cousin Tracy said to her during an argument. Tracy was at least 15 years older than Kayla. She had always had a vendetta against her younger cousin. For what? No one knew.

Kayla had had it hard growing up, and as an older cousin you'd think that she'd be more supportive and caring towards her younger cousin, but that was far from the case.

"You ain't going to graduate high school and will have a baby or two by the time you turn sixteen". More harsh words escaped her mouth as she went back and forth with Kayla. She had no shame about arguing with a child, because that's exactly what Kayla was to her. She had children who were only a few years younger than Kayla. She should have been ashamed of herself. As the adult, she should have showed some restraint.

Even though she was younger, Kayla held her own, hitting Tracy with some hurtful words herself. Kayla didn't know exactly why her older cousin always seemed to have an issue with her. Granted there were a few times Tracy felt as if Kayla was mean to her girls, but she had some bad kids. They would always hit Kayla and a few times she hit them right back. Tracy didn't like that, but at the same time she would never punish them for putting their hands on her when Kayla told her what they were doing. In addition to that, Lynn had to put Tracy in her place a time or two for talking to Kayla any type of way, and making threats. At the end of the day instead of being a big cousin and showing love, Tracy showed hatred towards her younger cousin more times than not. For the two cousins to have such a big gap in age, you sure couldn't tell.

For a short time, Kayla seemed to be at war with a few of her family members. Renay said she was mad at Kayla because she called the police to her house one day. Their cousin Rich was in from out of town visiting. He had been staying with Renay while he was in town. He and Anne's son, Twan, were close and he'd often let Twan drive his car. One day, Twan came over to Tish's apartment where Kayla was.

"Y'all want to go for a ride?" he asked.

The girls said yes, because they were just sitting around bored and talking. They went on a quick ride with Twan in Rich's car. When they came back, and hit the block. Rich was outside cussing and looking pissed off.

"Who told you to take my car little nigga," he said to Twan. Apparently, Rich hadn't given Twan permission to take his car. Twan decided to take it on his own while Rich was sleep. So Kayla went up to Renay's apartment after all the chaos outside. Rich was pissed off, and he started cursing Kayla out.

"I didn't know he didn't have permission," Kayla said to her cousin. Which was the truth, but he wasn't hearing what she had to say.

"Shut up," he demanded.

Kayla wasn't about to shut up—she didn't do anything wrong. So that's exactly what she said :"I ain't got to shut up." As soon as she said that Rich got up and smacked her in the face so hard he left his hand print on her face. Kayla was shocked that he had hit her. She wasn't about to try to fight him. He was physically bigger and stronger than her. At the same time she wasn't about to let him just get away with putting his hands on her either. She left the apartment and went to the next building to her Aunt Darla's and called the police on him. During her call she made sure she let them know that he had a warrant for his arrest also.

She waited outside for the police to come. When they arrived, she told them what happened. They took pictures of her face because it was still red from his hard hit. Then they proceeded up to Renay's apartment to get Rich. They came back down stating that everyone said he wasn't there.

"That's a lie," Kayla said knowing that he hadn't left. His car was still there and she had been outside the whole time waiting on the police. There was only one way in and one way out of the building, so she was sure he was still in there. The police escorted her to the apartment so she could identify him. "There he is right there," she said as the door opened and he sat right there on the couch. Everyone looked at her as if they were shocked that she pointed him out. Rich even had a shocked look that Kayla had told on him. She didn't care, he had no right to put his hands on her, but he did anyway. In her eyes he deserved to go to jail.

Once they arrested him and took him downtown, Renay called Kayla to curse her out. "You wrong for that. He hit Twan the same way and he didn't call the police," she said as if that was justification for what he did.

"I'm not Twan," Kayla let her know. The two passed a few words back and forth and just like that they weren't talking to each other anymore . That lasted for a few weeks until Renay finally saw Kayla and said, "Is this over with?"

Kayla was her go-to babysitter and had been since she lived in Hilltop projects. She couldn't stay mad at her forever.

— 16 —
FIGHT ON THE 48

Kayla called her people from school, to see what was going on. Her plan was to go hang out on the 48 after school instead of going home.

When she called, she found out that her cousin Renay had gotten into a fight with her neighbors. Renay had kicked in the people's door. After Kayla got the 411 on what was going down, she decided that she couldn't wait for school to be over. She was leaving right then and there to get in the action.

It had been a long time coming but the neighbors had been asking for some drama. The older woman who lived in the same apartment complex was always talking shit out the side of her neck, and her niece was always right there cosigning with her fat ass. Eventually something was bound to happen, and today was the day.

It all started over loud music early in the morning. Renay always played music while she cleaned up her house. So she was doing her usual and was apparently bothering her downstairs neighbors. Camille, the neighbor's niece who should have been in somebody's school, was the only one home.

She decided to grab a broom and bang on the ceiling screaming, "Shut the fuck up, people are trying to sleep." Renay heard the yelling over the music.

So she cut it down and screamed back, "Bitch, you could have just asked politely". That exchange quickly went left, and words started flying back and forth. To the point that Renay came up to her apartment into the hallway to talk shit. Camille kept talking shit too, but stayed in the apartment behind the locked door. She wasn't ready for or expecting what happened next.

Renay kicked the door in like she was the police conducting a raid. Her anger gave her more adrenaline and strength, and with two good kicks she was in the apartment. She attacked Camille, who was no longer talking shit and was no match for Renay. The fight went on for a minute or two before some of the other neighbors broke it up. No one called the police because Camile was a runaway. However, Renay had fucked her leg up kicking in the door so she went to the emergency room.

It took Kayla about an hour to get up on the 48 from Central High School on the bus. Nothing was going on when she arrived. Everybody was still talking about what had just popped off. However Kayla, Keisha, and Jackie stayed at Renay's apartment waiting, just in case there were any additional problems.

There weren't any until the smart mouth aunt came home. Kayla and Keisha were sitting on the porch talking to JJ and Bo and some of the other hood niggas that hung out up there.

"I wish a bitch would," the lady said out of nowhere. So everybody just looked at her as if she was crazy and laughed it off. Kayla on the other hand went upstairs to Renay's apartment. She looked around and started to plug up the iron to get it hot and take it downstairs for protection just in case the woman thought about doing something. Then she turned and looked at the entertainment cabinet that was full of empty Paul Mason bottles ranging in sizes. She grabbed a fifth, which was the biggest bottle there.

She put it inside her coat. The aunt was out there talking more shit about what she was gonna do and how she was gonna do it. Without a thought Kayla swung her coat back and straight hit her upside her head with the bottle. Once she hit her, she kept on swinging. The woman had a big frame like a linebacker, so she came falling forward on to Kayla knocking her off the small porch. The bottle fell but Kayla kept on swinging. The lady tried to fight back, but Keisha and Hope jumped in wildly swinging and hitting the woman. She had no chance that day.

Bo and JJ broke the fight up. The lady had blood dripping from her head; the bottle Kayla hit her with had broken the skin.

The police were called, but by the time they got there Kayla and Keisha had hit the other block and where at Trina's apartment awaiting for them to leave so they could go back for another round. That time they went back with Jackie, and low and behold the woman was still outside talking shit with the gash on her head.

So round two started, and all three of the girls attacked her at the same time. She was getting hit from every which way.

— 17 —

SENIOR YEAR

Ray and Mecca were not on good terms for a while. Kayla got tired of her dad's shenanigans. They'd pack their stuff up and move back to her granny's house. Then a few days later they'd be packing again moving right back to Mecca's. It was getting old and she was tired of the back and forth. So the next time it had happened, Mecca told her that she didn't have to leave if she didn't want to. Legally she wasn't supposed to, because Mecca was her guardian—not Ray.

Kayla took Mecca up on her offer and decided to stay. She figured Ray would be back in a few days anyway. However, days turned into weeks, and he seemed to be gone for good. Kayla started staying gone as well. She started staying the night with Jackie in Lynn's scattered-site housing unit. Lynn had recently moved out of town for good to Minnesota. Jackie didn't want to move so she stayed behind.

Mecca would come and give Kayla money from the check she received monthly for her. She was originally giving the money to Ray in order for him to pay his back child support, but since they were at odds she decided to give the money to Kayla. As the summer came closer to an end, Kayla decided that she didn't want to go back to Mecca's. When the opportunity came for Kayla to leave. It was a no brainer for her especially since Ray wasn't currently living there. So she reached out to her caseworker who made arrangements for her to live with Jackie.

Kayla and Jackie went house hunting and found a little house on the corner of 40th and Pratt. It wasn't fancy—it was honestly a little run down—but they were excited to move into something they could call their own. During that time, Keisha made her way back to Omaha to stay with them. She had originally left with Lynn, but she wasn't feeling Minnesota and wanted to come back to Omaha.

Three women living together was challenging at times. Jackie, Keisha, and Kayla had a close bond; they considered themselves all sisters rather than sisters and cousins. At times the littlest things irritated them about each other, and that bond was constantly tested. Jackie worked full time and Kayla went to school all day. Keisha had the luxury of staying at home all day, sleeping in, and not having a care in the world.

When it came to helping out around the house as far as cleaning and taking turns cooking dinner, Keisha didn't often put in her share. Kayla would come home from school and always have to clean up. Eventually the two cousins started to bump heads. Kayla got tired of trying to do it all by herself; and if she didn't do it, he knew she'd hear Jackie's mouth when she got home from work.

One day she got fed up and came home and didn't lift a finger. That was the wrong move.

As soon as Jackie got home, she started bitching, "Clean my mothafuckin house."

"But…" Kayla started to plead her case, but Jackie wasn't hearing it. She went on and on yelling and over talking Kayla. Kayla just went ahead and started to clean up, but she did it with an attitude.

Keisha never contributed to the upkeep of the house, but she made sure she got up every day, got dressed, and did her hair. She was sitting pretty in a dirty house. In addition to issues with the upkeep of the house, Jackie had a tendency to proclaim it was her house whenever she got mad about something. Although her name was on the list, it was all of their house.

The check Jackie received for Kayla every month covered the bills, and the money she went to work for was hers to do as she pleased. Keisha had income that she contributed to the household bills every month as well.

None of that mattered when Jackie was upset,"This my house," was all Kayla and Keisha heard. They learned to block Jackie out at times. She once even had the nerve to lock them out of the house while she left. They had a trick for that though—they climbed right through one of the back windows and politely let themselves back in.

For the most part it was cool living together. It was always a kicking it session. Just like anywhere else they had lived, they quickly got to know the neighborhood and the neighbors. Kayla knew this dude Darius from middle school at McMillan, and he lived in the neighborhood.

She and Darius started hanging out, and he introduced Keisha to his brother Derick. They hit it off, but Derick was one disrespectful person. He quickly rubbed Kayla the wrong way with his disrespect. Kayla wasn't the type to sit up and be disrespected by no man. She was always ready to go and stand up for herself. Her snap back was quick and she always ended up going toe-to-toe, round-for-round with a nigga for her respect.

Kayla's crew weren't as feisty as her; they let things slide. Kayla, on the other hand, didn't joke or play around like that.

Nothing about being disrespected by a man was funny to her. She and her crew could sit up all day and call each other bitch—it was like a term of endearment. When a man did it, it had a whole different feeling and vibe. Due to Kayla's unwillingness to take disrespect, she often got into it with the niggas that came around. Thanks to Derick, Kayla and Darius ended up breaking things off. Kayla couldn't deal with his brother, and Darius sided with his brother because that was his blood.

So the two broke up, and ended up going their separate ways. However, Keisha continued to deal with Derick, and he continued to come over to the house and irritate Kayla's soul. She couldn't stand his arrogant ass, but she was forced to deal with him on a regular basis. That caused Kayla and Keisha to fall out with each other after a while. They went over two months living in the same house and not speaking to one another.

Soon, Kayla made it to her last year of high school. She had just 10 more months of high school left, after all she had been through. Living with Jackie and Keisha had given her more freedom than she ever had before. There was no need to sneak off or stay out late. The fun was allowed to come directly to her.

Jackie sometimes got into her moods and would proclaim, "This is my house," but she did it so much Kayla and Keisha eventually became numb to it. They even warned their guests prior to them visiting of Jackie and her attitude.

Kayla was turning 17 and she and Jackie shared birth signs. They both were Virgos, so they decided to have a joint house party. There was a party almost every day at their house, but this was going to be the first official party. They invited everybody, all their friends and family. They cooked up some food, and brought liquor. The party ended up being a success until Ricky came through drunk and ruined it for everybody. He came in the house with a milk jug filled with vodka.

"You want some, you want some?" Ricky asked everyone in the house. Everyone declined, then he came in the kitchen and asked Kayla, who also declined.

Then he pushed, "Come on try it," and started pouring the jug of liquor onto her face. She got pissed off at him, and her whole outfit was ruined.

— 18 —
RECONNECTING & FALLING OUT AGAIN

Since transitioning from the projects to hanging around up on 48th street more often, Kayla, Jackie, and Keisha hadn't seen much of their old friends. Kayla missed her play daughter Liyah. Liyah was Shaun's daughter that she took a liking to when she used to babysit for her a few years prior.

Thanks to Williemae, a butch chick from Spencer, Shaun had once again gotten mad at Kayla and stopped speaking with her. Williemae made Shaun believe that Kayla was flirting with her boyfriend, Bam. That was the furthest thing from the truth, but with Kayla's history, Shaun easily believed the lie.

Jackie and Kayla were chilling at Lisa's house one day listening to music. Williemae who was staying with Lisa at the time was asleep on the couch. Bam was in the kitchen eating. Busta Rhymes and Janet Jackson's song, "What's It Gonna Be" came on the radio, and Kayla started dancing to the song. Williemae, who was "sleeping" on the couch, decided to tell Shaun that Kayla was bouncing her ass in front of Bam. Now Shaun was mad at her all over again.

"You are always messing with somebody man," Shaun said to Kayla. No matter what Kayla said Shaun didn't believe her. So Kayla stopped trying to explain herself. She knew what she did and did not do. Bam was not her type of man. He was a bum using Shaun just like the rest of the men she had dealt with. When Kayla met Bam he was staying in the abandoned empty project unit next to her aunt Lynn. He called himself a pimp, but didn't have two dimes to rub together, Even Jackie backed her cousin up, but Shaun still wasn't trying to hear it. That was the last time Kayla had seen or heard from Shaun.

Regardless of how Kayla felt about Shaun, she had love for her daughter, Liyah. The little girl was like her own. Kayla happened to be going to school at Central with Shaun's cousin, so she reached out to her for Shaun's number. Kayla didn't know how the conversation would go, but she was willing to try just to see Liyah. So she made the call.

To her surprise, Shaun was willing to forgive and forget, and open to letting Kayla see Liyah. They stayed right up the street and around the corner on 46th and Bedford. With that one phone call everybody became cool again. Shaun started coming over kicking it, she had had another baby since the last time they had seen her. They had heard about the scandal behind her new son. She had him by this girl Ke Ke's husband. Ke Ke would fight Shaun every time she saw her, but that didn't stop her from fucking around with her man.

For a while everything was cool between them, like nothing had ever happened, until her homegirl, Butter, randomly decided to start some shit. Butter stayed in the area too and she would often come over to the house and hang out. One day Shaun called and wanted someone to meet her halfway while she walked over. It just so happened that Butter was on the other line trying to get over to the house too.

"Why don't you meet Shaun, and y'all come together," Kayla suggested to Butter.

"Ain't nobody trying to be walking with no kids, shit I'm trying to be cute," she replied. Kayla laughed at Butter's comment, and that was it. Well that conversation went back to Shaun but, Butter exchanged her statement for Kayla's.

As usual, Shaun was quick to get mad at Kayla, and she confronted Kayla with the information. Kayla tried to tell the real story—the truth—but like always no one was trying to hear her. Kayla hated the fact that she was the youngest. Everyone thought they could just come at her and talk to her any kind of way. But this time, she snapped back on Shaun. She didn't care how the situation ended. She wasn't going to keep getting talked to like a little kid. She may have been the youngest, but none of them females were her momma. She didn't even let her momma talk to her crazy.

That small situation got dragged out and turned into a bigger issue than it should have. Out of anger, Kayla told Shaun about her trifling self. Kayla was the one who made sure her daughter was able to celebrate her birthday. Shaun had given her so-called nigga her money to go flip, and he never came back. The day of Liyah's birthday, Shaun was sitting around waiting on this nigga to show and he never did. She had a house full of kids waiting on a birthday party, and he wouldn't even answer his phone. Eventually she came to realization that he wasn't coming, so she called Kayla who came through. She got Liyah and brought her a birthday gift, cake and ice cream and threw her a personal party at her house.

Kayla wasn't a kid that day, when she came through for Shaun's daughter. There was always a beef between Shaun and Kayla from that day forward, however, Shaun and

Jackie remained cool. That meant Kayla had to see her damn near every day, because she was always over there needing something. Needing some food, needing to borrow some money, needing a cigarette. She was always needing something, because whatever she did have she was giving to a nigga.

— 19 —

BLOOD THICKER THAN WATER?

After Kayla's graduation, Jackie decided it was time to move out of their little raggedy house on the hill. The landlord was ghetto and never wanted to fix any thing. He was living in a nice ass house down in the Carter Lake area, but he was a slum lord. The ceiling in the living room had fallen, and he didn't even come out to fix that. Living there was fun for a while, and it served its initial purpose, but it was time to go.

They ended up finding a house a few blocks away off Pinkney street. It was nice and definitely an upgrade from where they were moving from. Once they got moved in, they had to break the house in just like everywhere else they went. It was in the same neighborhood, so they pretty much knew everybody, but they quickly caught the attention of the dudes who stayed across the street. Ike and Derick, two high yellow young dudes. They befriended them in no time at all.

They had a small get together within the first week of moving in, and their new friends from across the street were in attendance. They partied all night long smoking weed and drinking Seagram's Gin. Jackie's childhood friend Nikki came over and got sloppy drunk and was telling Jackie's secrets from back in the days when they were Kayla's and Keisha's age.

The next morning was Father's Day, so Kayla got up early to call Ray and wish him a Happy Father's Day. She was the only one awake in the house. Jackie and Keisha were down for the count. As she was in the tub she heard somebody knocking at the door. So from the bathroom window she yelled "who is it".

"Shaun."

Since everyone was asleep and she was in the tub, she said just that –"Everybody asleep." Then she continued with her bath.

Kayla went downstairs to get dressed and she heard the house phone ringing. It was Shaun crying to Jackie that she had come over and Kayla wouldn't let her in. Crying about how she had her son and it was hot outside. In all reality she either needed a ride, or came to bum a cigarette.

Next thing she knew Jackie was at the top of the stairs yelling, "Kayla, did Shaun come over here this morning?"

"Yeah she did."

"Well why you didn't let her in?"

"Because, I was in the tub."

Jackie got to yelling and cursing Kayla out, "You don't do my friends like that".

Kayla was confused. "Do your friends like what" Kayla questioned.

"You was asleep, and I was in the tub," she said again because it was as simple as that. "What was I supposed to do jump out the tub to let her in?" Kayla asked seriously. "It's funny how she can call now. She should have called before she just came over," Kayla said snapping back at Jackie. Kayla and Jackie went back and forth arguing. Jackie didn't like the fact that Kayla was talking back, so Jackie threw the cordless phone down the stairs at Kayla. It hit her in her ankle and broke skin. Kayla looked down at her foot and saw blood. She couldn't believe that her cousin had actually just thrown the phone at her. Jackie had made a big deal out of nothing. Kayla's first reaction was to call the police on Jackie, who heard Kayla on the phone with the 911 operator. Jackie grabbed her car keys and left the house.

The police came, but since Jackie had left they couldn't do anything about it. Kayla was sitting on the porch when Jackie finally pulled back up about an hour later with her Shaun in the car. She went in the house and told Keisha to come with her.

Then she made sure she told Kayla, "This is my house," as she locked the doors and pulled off. Kayla was in disbelief at how her cousin was acting and treating her. Kayla called her aunt Marie and told her what was going on, and Marie came immediately to get her niece. Kayla was pissed off and hurt at the same time. She didn't do anything wrong. While Kayla was waiting she made sure she left Jackie something to remember her by. She carved the word BITCH in all capital letters with a 4-way tire iron on her door, and broke out the kitchen window.

～

Just a few weeks prior, everything seemed to be going fine. Kayla was sitting in her chair during the commencement. For a moment, she had blocked out all the commotion, and it was all a blur as she replayed moments of her life. She recalled a lot of good times, such as birthday parties, family gatherings. Her fondest memory was of Kay and her old bedtime routine. Every night before bed they'd tell each other "goodnight" and give each other a kiss, hug, and say "I love you".

Then there were the not so good memories of people in her family telling her "You're going to be just like your momma," or "By the time you turn 16, you will have 2 kids".

Those thoughts played in her mind as she was waiting for her name to be called. Her thoughts had her so emotional that she almost cried, but she held back the tears. She replaced her tears with a smile because she had beaten all the odds against her. She was about to graduate in front of her loved ones. She had family and friends there cheering her on showing her support.

Finally it was her row's turn to stand. Kayla couldn't hold back her smile. She was grinning from ear to ear showing off her dimples as she walked that stage and received her diploma.

JUST LIKE DADDY

——————◢——————

They say that every girl's first love is her daddy. Trina was no different from any other girl. She was a daddy's girl. He was her first love—she admired everything about her daddy. His word was his bond, and she trusted him more than she trusted anyone else.

From the time she could remember anything, she remembered her daddy. Like most men, Raymond wanted a boy, but at the very moment he found out the news that he was having a daughter his life changed forever. He would do anything to protect her. In the beginning her showered her with love and attention, and spent all his free time with his baby girl.

As the years passed, he didn't get to spend as much quality time that he would have liked with her. So, he made up for the lack time by replacing it with cash and gifts. He showered his baby girl with gifts all the time. Trina associated her dad with money and gifts, and that was enough to keep her happy.

As she started getting older turning from a little girl to a young lady, their relationship took a 360 turn around. He wasn't ready for his little girl to grow up. He was afraid that she'd come across men like himself. That was the Karma he wasn't ready for. He had done his share of womanizing, and he knew firsthand the type of men that were in this world. Those men were out there just lurking and preying over young girls like his Trina. He didn't know how to react to his baby girl growing up. So, during her most vulnerable time while she was coming of age he disappeared.

When Trina started dating, she went for a certain type of man. Her main requirement was that he had to have money to buy her gifts to show her love. Where she came from, the only men with money were the neighborhood hustlers just like her daddy…

Just Like Daddy /2020

Makayla's favorite quotes:

"Your past doesn't have to determine your future."

"Never judge a book by its cover."

ABOUT THE AUTHOR

Makayla LaShawn Townsell was born in Omaha, Nebraska, on September 22, 1983, to parents Susan Townsell and Kevin Brewer. She was blessed with two other women to call mom or "other mother," Carolyn Townsell and Lori Hill. Makayla has two known siblings, Breonna and Tyrone, both on her father's side, and a nephew, Devron, and my niece Le'Auni.

Makayla graduated from Central High School on May 22, 2001. On May 10, 2012, she graduated from Metropolitan Community College with an Associate of Arts Administrative Assistant degree. Makayla has earned her Bachelor's degree in Business from Bellevue University.

She is the mother of four: Lafayette, LaMar'e, Kevin, and Kaylee, and is engaged to the father of her children, Dawawn.

Makayla aspires to be a great writer, such as her favorites, Tracy McMillan, Eric Jerome Dickey, and the late Maya Angelou.

Her hope is to end the cycle of staying silent and keeping secrets, or, at a bare minimum, raise awareness. "TELL SOMEBODY!"

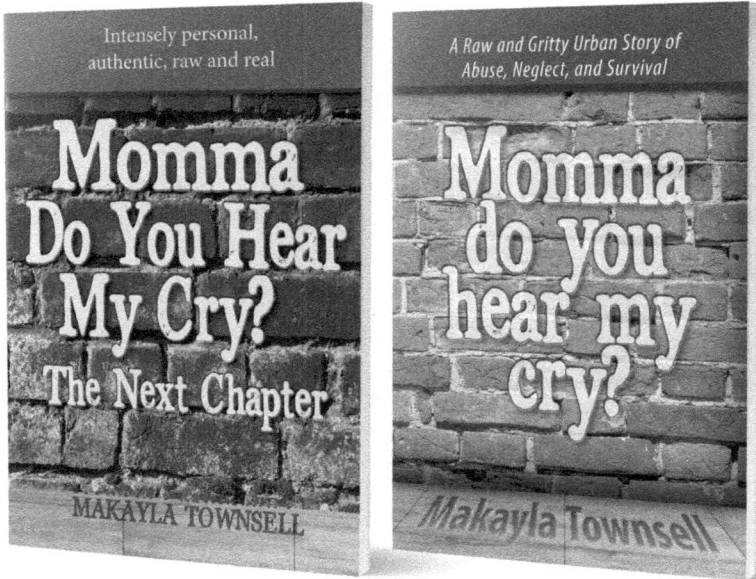

Find Momma Do You Hear My Cry? (Book 1)
and Momma Do You Hear My Cry? The Next Chapter (Book 2)
at www.GBattlesPublishing.com and Amazon.com
or order from your favorite bookseller.